D0190052

HIRE
POWER

HIRE
POWER

The 6-Step Process
to Get the Job You Need
in 60 Days—Guaranteed!

Irv Zuckerman

A PERIGEE BOOK

Perigee Books
are published by
The Putnam Publishing Group
200 Madison Avenue
New York, NY 10016

Copyright © 1993 by Zuckerman Foundation, Inc.

All rights reserved. This book, or parts thereof,
may not be reproduced in any form without permission.
Published simultaneously in Canada

Library of Congress Cataloging-in-Publication Data

Zuckerman, Irv.
    Hire power : the 6-step process to get the job you need in 60
days—guaranteed! / Irv Zuckerman.
        p.   cm.
    ISBN 0-399-51824-X (acid-free paper)
    1. Job hunting—United States. I. Title.
HF5382.75.U6Z83   1993   93-942 CIP
650.14—dc20

Cover design by Terrence Fehr
Cover photo © by Barbara & Co.

Printed in the United States of America
1 2 3 4 5 6 7 8 9 10

This book is printed on acid-free paper.

To Claire, for all the good questions

Dear Reader:

Here's the deal:

If there were such a thing as a sex manual for job-seeking, *Hire Power* would be it. Both parties to the job-search—the one looking to be hired and the one with the power to say yes—can read these pages and benefit. That's because there are no trick strategies designed to manipulate each other.

What you'll find in this book is a 6-Step Job-Getting Process that works because it establishes an honest communication between you and the people who can offer you a job. The only time it fails is when the job-seeker leaves something out. Any omission alters the Process, and when you alter a process you naturally alter the result.

This means that if you follow the Process, step by step, you'll wind up with a job offer. If not, I will give back the purchase price of this book. All I want in exchange for this guarantee is a copy of what you did. That way, I can locate what went wrong.*

Of course, if you wind up getting a great job, send me your success story. You won't get a refund, but it's the least I deserve for sticking my neck out this way. Don't you agree?

Are you:

• Out of a job because you got axed?

* See the back of the book for details on the Money Back Guarantee.

- In a job that you don't particularly like or where your talents are underemployed?
- In a job you like, but at a dead end?

And have you:

- Used up all your Contacts?
- Sent a resume to everyone you could think of?
- Gotten weary (or wary) of hearing NO yet again?

Good. You're ready. Let's start from there.

Irv Zuckerman

CONTENTS

THE OVERVIEW

It is time to face up to the fact that no matter which side of the aisle runs this country, the economy may never again be able to provide a good job for everyone. That's both bad news and good news. It's bad news for the people who can't or don't want to learn to compete for the remaining seats in the current round of professional musical chairs. They quit. Which is good news for those who *do* want to learn. They win.

This book will teach you how to compete for a job. As any professional in any other form of competition will tell you, clever tricks and sly techniques don't get it done. What it takes, and what the 6-Step Job-Getting Process teaches, is careful preparation.

What the Process cannot teach, however, is attitude. If you had sat in on one of our sessions over the past eight years, you would have learned what experience has shown to be the three basic reasons for self-defeat:

- Embarrassment
- Defensiveness
- Passivity

Fred celebrated his fourteenth anniversary at the bank by getting fired. Nothing wrong with his work—it's just that his organization was centralizing its operation in another city. There was nothing wrong with his skills, either. As he found out during his participation in the Process, they were readily marketable. But the embarrassment of having been dumped while others of lesser talent had been kept on immobilized him—made him deaf to any positive possibilities.

The only successful treatment was to use the kind of in-your-face language that identified embarrassment for what it really was—self-pity in a nicer suit. That's why every word in this text keeps its eye on the goal: to help you get the kind of job you want as soon as you can possibly get it.

When Fred started he felt undervalued and overaged. Now when he refers to the Process he'll tell you, "You don't have to love what it says. You just have to *do* what it says."

Anne was a single parent with four children. Her job paid her about half of what she needed and what her skills could command. But no matter what action the Process recommended, her response was defensive: "That wouldn't work for me." What Anne was really saying was that it was too much work for her. The step-by-step Process takes effort—the kind of effort she may never have expended before. Which is why she was stuck in a dead-end job.

What changed Anne's attitude and moved her in a more positive direction was just that—direction. Instead of suggesting, the Process insisted. So, as you go through the material, you may feel a finger in your chest from time to time. It's intentional.

After three or four interviewers had told Steve that at fifty-three he was too old, he began to believe it. He came to the course looking for a support group that would make him feel OK about giving up and waiting for things to get better. What he got was a kick in the ass just hard enough to clear his vision.

He was able to see the difference between the disadvantage of his age and the advantage of the extra skills those years had brought him.

Steve called the language you'll be reading a "jump-start." You can call it what you like, as long as it does for you what it did for him.

Instead of the usual chapter format, this book is divided into the six steps of the Job-Getting Process:

Step 1: Learn how to create a

WORD BANK

of 200 Words that best describe your most important achievement and demonstrate your skills.

Step 2: Learn how to use your WORD BANK to create the kind of

SELF-PRESENTATION

that will initiate professional discussions with people who can help you match your skills to the criteria of the job you want.

Step 3: Learn how to ask the one question that best initiates a

CONTACT CONVERSATION

from which you learn the criteria you must meet to get the job you want.

Step 4: Learn how to create a

COMPETITIVE RESUME

that draws on your WORD BANK to match the criteria of the job you want.

Step 5: Learn how to conduct a

COMPETITIVE JOB INTERVIEW

that demonstrates your ability to best meet each of the job criteria.

Step 6: Learn how to develop a

POST-INTERVIEW PROCEDURE

that keeps the odds in your favor despite other candidates or interviewers.

INTRODUCTION

What if job opportunities were played out like a tennis match with all the competitors pitted against each other in an elimination tourney? Can't you just see it? A lot of sweating and grunting while, in the stands, families and friends yell advice and encouragement.

When the final scores are posted, it's all over. Cheers for the victor and a place among the employed. Cameras click and microphones record that first moment of elation that comes with hearing the two most important words in today's America: "You're hired."

And for the losers? Form letters of consolation. Promises to keep their names on file. Maybe an announcement of the date of the next competition, which in this economic climate may be called because of rain.

To a professional competitor, however, losing is a signal that something has to change. When you're not as good as the winner, you've got to get better or get out of the game. But if you're competing for a job you need, getting out of the game isn't an option. You've got to get better.

True, you can get "experts" to help you create a better resume. Or you can get friends or agencies to set up the Contacts that might get you interviews. But sooner or later it's up to you and you alone. From the moment you cross the threshold of the Decision-Maker's office to start that awkward foreplay of introductions, maybe listening to an apology for lateness-but-something-came-up, and an invitation to sit down and make yourself comfortable (as if that were possible under the circumstances), it's all up to you. Instead of blowing your next opportunity, you want to get hired. OK. Here's how:

First, what is a blown opportunity?

There are the jobs you are wrong for, that you shouldn't be considered for in the first place. Determining that and deciding to bow out is not a blown opportunity. There are jobs that are wrong for you, even though you can do them. Finding that out and taking your leave is also not a blown opportunity.

What is? Let's screen out the music and the background chatter and eavesdrop on the guy on the next bar stool:

FRIEND: *How'd it go at Multinational Enterprises this morning?*

GUY: *Well, I'll tell you in a minute. Bartender, another one of these, and easy on the ice this time. Thanks. How'd it go? Well, it didn't. For one thing, I've seen a lot of department managers in my day, but this one, believe me, was a real horse's ass. Wouldn't know talent if it fell on him. I was perfect for that job—just the right experience. You could see that the more I told him about myself, the more antsy he got. Probably thought I was after his spot. Not that I couldn't have done it, believe me. A real horse's ass. Here, have another.*

That was a blown opportunity. Anytime you fit the job specs and can prove it, are willing to take the dollars offered, feel that it's the right spot for you, and weren't made an offer, you blew it. You can go through a whole song and dance about having made the first cut, having gone all the way to the top where it was between you and a combination of Einstein, Schweitzer, and Pasteur, or that the Decision-Maker was a horse's ass, but the sad fact is staring you in the face. You blew it.

During good times, what-the-hell. There are more jobs open than there are talented people to fill them. Another opportunity will be along any minute. But how about when times are temporarily tight due to a worsening economic situation? Or how about when times are permanently tight because your age, color, sex, or accent is not exactly what the Decision-Makers had in mind? During those times when you blow the opportunity, you also blow a Contact that may be irreplaceable.

Taking responsibility means being mature enough to face certain realities. In a period of thinning down and cutting back, management's first thought is of firing, not hiring. Landing one of the available spots calls for competitive preparation—a return to the basic three-R's:

RESEARCH: *In plain language, this means doing your homework. If you neglect to learn as much about the company as you can and they wind up filling the job from within or hiring somebody else, don't assign that spot on the end of the horse to anyone but yourself.*

REHEARSE: *When the rest of your life may hang in the balance of one hour in the Decision-Maker's office, forget spontaneity. We may be born with the instincts for sex, but it takes a certain amount of practice to become really good at it. In the same way, you may be born with the instinct to communicate, but without sufficient preparation you're bound to make mistakes.*

REVIEW: *There are just six steps outlined in this text—each tested under fire. If you're reading this page, it's a sign that you're looking for a job or trying to get a better one. And your first attempt may be all you need. But suppose you miss? It's important to be able to look at the experience objectively. Don't bend too far forward to take bows you don't deserve. Nor should you bend over backward to be overcritical. This book will help you locate the omissions and commissions that may have cost you. Then, next time, you'll be more competitive.*

GETTING READY

DEVELOPING A COMPETITIVE ATTITUDE

Too much of what we see and hear gives the idea of competition a bad name. Films like *Wall Street* portray financial carnivores who feed off each other's vitals. Contact sports feature people who wound in order to win. Not to mention the idiot who cuts in front of your car without signaling so that he could beat you to the toll booth.

How to live with the more competitive side of yourself

But competition is the name of this game. Whoever hires you is going to reject or maybe even fire somebody else. That is a discomforting thought to some people.

Job-getting is, in fact, the most competitive activity around. There are no wild-card applicants, purses for runners-up, or chants of "Wait till next year" to comfort the losers. So if you have trouble "talking about yourself" or "selling yourself" or "blowing your own horn," it's time to exercise your lips.

How to understand the difference between being an optimist and a pessimist

Learning how to do better at job-getting, like learning how to do better at anything, suggests change. After all, how can anything get better if every element within it remains the same? There may be times as you're reading this book, when something will be asked of you and you say, "I can't do that." And you'd be right. You can't. But it's *how* you say it that indicates whether you're an optimist or a pessimist.

If you're a pessimist you'll say, "I can't do that *because . . .*" and come up with a dozen reasons why not. Some of your reasons will reflect a valid lack of confidence. Others are there simply to provide a needed excuse in case you blow it. The word "because" helps to move a self-fulfilling prophecy neatly into place.

If you're an optimist you might also say, "I can't do that." Being an optimist doesn't rule out being a realist. But the next word isn't "because." It's "unless."

"I can't do that *unless* I get the chance to prepare in advance" suggests that while you're optimistic about the outcome, you'd feel a lot more comfortable with the idea if you could rehearse. In the same way, "I can't do that unless I have more help with . . ." is an optimistic appraisal of your present skills and a recognition of your need for help to improve.

If you're an optimist (or can develop that attitude), you're in luck. Those who have used the Process over the years have come up with a great many "unless's" that will probably work for you. And they're all recorded here.

How to keep yourself on the hook, instead of laying the blame for what's happening (or not happening) on others

This calls for maintaining the attitude that whatever happens during your job-getting efforts is something *you* helped to bring about. This goes for the good news as well as the bad.

First, the good news. You did some careful research. You asked the right questions. This means you knew enough about your Target organization to direct the key points of your skills and experience to the bull's-eye. You were on the Inside Track. This doesn't mean automatic success, but it does mean you know how. And once you know how, success is a matter of persistence.

Now, the bad news. You said or did all the wrong things. Or you didn't say or do enough of the right things. This doesn't mean that you have no talent or that you're a loser. It means you made a mistake. Mistakes, as you will see, are there to be reviewed and corrected.

But if you hear yourself saying, "I didn't get the job because they or he or she . . ." watch out. You're letting yourself off the hook—which is like letting the steam out of your determination to work a little smarter next time. Instead, take the blame. What was it that you could have done better . . . with more accuracy . . . with more effort? It's there, somewhere.

How to keep your eye on your goal by avoiding such distracting side issues as "showing" your family, your ex-boss, etc.

Your goal is to get the job you want. That's it. If you're out to prove that your previous employer was wrong in failing to promote you or in letting you go, forget it. If you're out to relieve the anxiety of family or friends or whatever gods may be who want you to be a success, save it. These are distractions that can only get in your way.

In fact, don't even talk about what you're doing. People will have only one of three reactions—none of which are particularly helpful:

REACTION #1: *"You're doing what? That sounds pretty hokey to me."*

That kind of response can't help but put you on the defensive. Pretty soon you're trying to explain what it is you're doing and why you're doing it to people who aren't thinking along the same lines you are. You're going to sound uncertain to them—and to yourself. Pretty soon your self-confidence is back to square one. Avoid it.

REACTION #2: *"What's new about that? Those ideas have been around for years!"*

Not really. What you're about to discover are the separate elements of a total Process. Some may look familiar. But unless we have worked together in some previous existence, chances are you have never taken all the steps that work together in a specific sequence to get you the results you're looking for. If you had done so, you would now be enjoying the job you have and would not be reading this page.

REACTION #3: *"How are you getting on with your job hunt?"*

If the constant repetition of this question doesn't get on your nerves, you don't have any. And if you're out of a job and have a desperate need to find one, being nervous about it can sap your confidence. So can the worried looks people give you when you tell them what you're doing and they fail to understand it.

How *do* you handle the anxieties of well-wishers? It's easy enough to say that their anxieties are their problem, not yours. Even the realization that some well-wishers don't really wish you all that well may not help. And it's not going to make you feel any better to be rude to family or friends. So, if they do ask, answer their questions with a question of your own: "Since you brought up my job-search, let me ask you: Whom do you know that I can talk to in the field of (computer science, insurance, laser holography, animal husbandry, retailing, etc.)?" Those who really want to help you might stop asking questions about how you're doing and start helping you to do better. Those who don't . . . well, nothing gives you breathing room with some people quite as fast as asking them for help.

ORGANIZING YOUR JOB-GETTING CAMPAIGN

Remember, job-getting, particularly in a bad market, is America's most competitive activity. So before you begin, you'll need a scorecard listing the various working parts and participants, as well as the role each plays in your future:

1) The Process. This is the 6-Step persuasion that includes everything from initial homework to final handshake. Too many people think poorly of the ability to persuade. They look upon it as a series of "techniques" with which skilled manipulators can "trick" an unsuspecting Decision-Maker into mak-

ing a decision he/she might not have made with a less-clouded mind. Wrong on two counts:

First, if you were that skilled at manipulating others, how come you don't already have the job you want?

Second, would you want to work for someone who is that easily fooled?

2) The Decision-Maker. He or she is the person who is going to decide whether you or someone else is chosen for the job you want. There may be more than one Decision-Maker providing the input that shapes the final decision, but as you'll see, that's no big deal.

3) The individual with the Inside Track. This is the someone else who wants the same job you're after and has the competitive edge. He or she may already work for the company in another capacity, may have the advantage of a network connection that is stronger than yours, or may be better at the three R's. For whatever reason, the Inside Track is the person they say yes to when they say no to you.

4) The Inside-Track Resume. It's aimed directly at the job in question. This is the most dangerous thing to appear on the Decision-Maker's desk—if it isn't yours. If it *is* yours, it's a danger to everyone else who has submitted a standard, "Buck-Shot" (BS) Resume that is little more than a menu of their work experience.

5) The Target organizations or industries you've selected as the best possible opportunities for you to put your skills to work. (Mind you, the term is *skills*, not experience. Experience is type-casting. From the moment you describe yourself as *being* something—banker, marketer, production manager—that's all you can be. Skills, however, describe not what

you are, but what you've done and what you can do. That's what Decision-Makers want to buy.)

For example, if you were working in the mortgage department of a bank and were let go because of consolidation, that may be a trend. Looking for another mortgage job may put a limit on your possibilities. If you prefer to stay in banking, you could look for other departments that might make use of your skills. Or you might target a wider area—looking at other industries that might make use of your skills. Or both.

6) The Contact. The person who gives you the kind of information you need about your Target organizations so that you can create not just one but a series of Inside-Track Resumes, depending on the kinds of jobs you're after. The more Contacts, the more likely you are to get the information you need—and the more likely you are to find a Decision-Maker among them.

7) The WORD BANK. A 200-word (more or less) account of your most important achievement that helps you to present the valuable skills you have to offer, rather than your experience, age, or previous condition of servitude.

The WORD BANK replaces the risky "tell-me-about-yourself" ad-lib, and becomes the foundation on which you build your new job-getting campaign. 200 words isn't many, which means that each must be carefully selected.

From then on, in every letter, phone conversation, or interview, you're ready to put your best words forward. If there is more than one achievement in your background, you'll need more than one edition.

8) The SELF-PRESENTATION. Face-to-face, in the mail or on the phone, you present your skills to every Contact who

might possibly help you get the information you need. Instead of the usual I'm-out-of-a-job-can-you-help-me message, which tends to send the people you want to contact "out of the office" or "away from their desks right now," your SELF-PRESENTATION has to contain the best of your 200 Words.

9) The CONTACT CONVERSATION. This is not the biggy. It's not going to end with a job offer. Start it with the one question that's going to provide the job criteria you need to know to prepare the Inside-Track Resume that will lead to the JOB INTERVIEW and the job offer.

10) The JOB INTERVIEW. This is the biggy but only one step of the Process—the proverbial tip of the iceberg. Without a solid base in place, it would melt without a trace. And if you've gotten that far and blown it, you've lost more than the job. You've lost a valuable contact and the time and effort that went into obtaining it.

11) The Job-Getter. That's you. Why not an applicant? Because "applicant" sounds too much like "supplicant," which suggests a hat-in-hand pleading for "a break." A Job-Getter, on the other hand, projects a more accurate image—one that says things like:

"Let me take the opportunity of this interview to convince you that I'm the person you should choose for this job."

"Tell me about the criteria for this job so that I can tell you how well I can meet them."

"There are so many advantages to hiring me that even if a job doesn't exist at present, it will pay you to create one."

12) The Feeling of Activity. If you had a job, you'd be working every day, right? In fact, if you had some kind of tough, high-pressure job you'd be working some nights and weekends as well. Can you imagine a tougher, more high-pressure job than finding a job in a tough market?

How to find a place to do your work-getting work

There's nothing more seductive than your home environment. Why not sleep an hour later? After all, you have "nothing to do." What's in the fridge? Where's the *TV Guide*? C'mon, give yourself a break. After all those years of loyal service to those ungrateful SOB's, you've got it coming.

When you start thinking that way, what you've got coming isn't a break. It's a breakdown. Is it because you have no boss to give you assignments? No deadlines? Wrong! Tape your rent or mortgage bill to your headboard. Tape your car payment on your TV screen. That should get you out of the house. But where to? After all, you have no interviews for that day.

Lean on friends who have businesses or firms where a desk is free. In this market there are bound to be more than a few. What does your friend get out of it? The good feeling that comes with helping a friend in need. In a more pragmatic sense, if it's the kind of firm where clients come visiting, one less empty office or desk looks better.

If you had the kind of job where you bought products or services, lean on your suppliers. They don't even have to be your friends. The sooner you're re-employed, the better for you—and maybe for them.

The term "lean" means a strong request. Don't beg. Ask. The worst that can happen is that they say no. No, that's not the worst that can happen. The worst is that they say yes and then regret it because you become such a pain in the neck. Promise that you won't. And don't.

You say you have no friends, no suppliers, no nothing? Then create an office in your home, with desk, files, and the professional environment you're looking for. True, it's isolated. True, it's too near the refrigerator and other distractions. But if you have the discipline to close the door and work steadily at getting work, it should do.

How to create a working persona even if you're not

When you had a job, you looked like it. Your dress, demeanor, and attitude were those of the working person. Just because you have no job doesn't mean you have no identity. If you used to have a business card, stationery, or memo paper that read "From the desk of . . ." get new ones. It isn't that expensive and, as you'll see later on, might even pay for itself in freelance or part-time work in your field.

Then set up a goal-oriented working routine.

You did it when you were employed. Now that you have a place to get phone calls, write letters and Inside-Track Resumes, you can do it again. Not on a hit-and-miss, let's-see-what-shall-I-do-today basis, but with a specific plan worked out with the help of this guide:

- What kind of job do I want?
- Where is it?
- How can I get the Inside Track?

How to be persuasive rather than aggressive

Too many books on the subject of job-getting see it as a contest between the Job-Seeker and the Decision-Maker, in which one side wins and the other loses. This is simply not true. Any competitive management knows it must deliver MORE. More profit. More productivity. More service. So management must hire competitive people who can help them to achieve these objectives. If you're the kind of person who can deliver more, it means you and the Decision-Maker are really on the same side. All you have to do now is persuade him/her that you can deliver.

Persuasion, like any good communication, is based on an honest exchange of information between you and the Decision-Maker. No tricks, no sudden, clever strategies, no adroit lies—on either side. You don't need to be aggressive— just well prepared.

Now, here comes yet another misapprehension. It rules that anything that is not totally spontaneous is somehow contrived and dishonest. So, by extension, any preparation—or, worse yet, rehearsal—of what you plan to say and do and how you plan to say and do it has the distinct odor of snake oil.

To prove how wrong that idea can be, think back to an important disappointment in your life—where the outcome depended on your ability to persuade some Decision-Maker to your point of view. You didn't succeed. After the interview, discussion, presentation, or confrontation, the job, order, budget, promotion, seat in the class, or love in the heart went to somebody else. No matter how easily you were let down, no matter how tactfully the "NO" was gift-wrapped, the result was the same. You "lost." Which suggests that whoever you went one-on-one with "won."

Isn't it then that the "shouldas" set in? Didn't you, in a cerebral instant replay, start thinking of what you shoulda said and how you shoulda said it? But it was too late, wasn't it? So what's wrong with thinking and planning ahead of time? What's wrong with establishing a Process that can help you become more persuasive by focusing on what the Decision-Maker is trying to achieve and how to persuade him or her that you're the one with the best skills to help achieve it?

STEP 1

Learn How to Create a
WORD BANK
of 200 Words That Best
Describe Your Most Important
Achievement and Demonstrate
Your Skills

Start by assembling the evidence that proves you have skills that make you worth talking to.

Remember, the term is *skills*, not experience. You want to describe not what you are, but what you've done and what you can do. That's what Decision-Makers want to buy. That's why the first step of the Process is to focus on your skills and what makes them competitive—if not superior—to those of anyone else the Decision-Maker may be considering.

ACCURACY IS FASTER THAN SPEED

You need a job right away. No. Sooner than right away. Maybe you've just gotten axed, and while your salary has stopped, your expenses haven't. Or maybe your golden handshake turned out to be iron pyrite. Or you have a job but feel your career is blocked. Every time an advancement appears on the horizon, so does a better candidate. Or the organization really provides little room for growth. Whatever the case, it's time to get into high gear and get the word out that you're looking. So you:

- Rush 100 resumes into the mail.
- Rush to list your name with every headhunter you can find.
- Rush to answer every ad you can find.

During a recession, that's the shortest road to a depression. Unless you're the kind who generally wins the lottery (and if that's the case what are you doing here?), you're going to get hit with more rejections than you ever thought existed.

You'll know that you've arrived at a full depression when you find yourself asking yourself, "Why me?" This is when you start wondering why the person for whom you worked so hard and has rewarded you by putting your name on the WCWDWL (whom-can-we-do-without list). True, they may have let the whole department, or office, or division, loose—including your boss. True, you may have sensed that the merger was coming or that there wasn't enough work to keep you busy but preferred to ignore the handwriting on the wall. But that's myopia, which is a correctable vision problem, not a negative comment on your skills or abilities.

How to organize your achievements so that they apply to a number of different fields

So turn the "Why me?" question on its head. Instead of "Why me? Why was I fired?" ask yourself, "Why me? Why should I be hired?" This will not only help you avoid depression, but will also turn the focus of the question to where it truly belongs: Why should your next employer hire you?

Good question—no matter how you read it.

- *Why* should your next employer hire you?
- Why *should* your next employer hire you?
- Why should *your* next employer hire you?
- Why should your *next* employer hire you?
- Why should your next employer hire *you*?

How to write a 200-word (more or less) account of your most important achievement

How you answer the "Why me?" question in your own head (later on, we'll get to how to answer it during an interview) is the first and most important action you'll take during your job-search.

To do so, you'll need some tools. That shouldn't surprise you. Every job needs tools of one kind or another. The nature of these particular tools, however, might. For maximum effectiveness, you'll need a black, felt-tipped pen and a yellow, legal-size pad. Why so specific? You'll find out. Until then, trust me.

At the top of the yellow, legal-size pad write (better yet, print) the words, "My Most Important Achievement Was . . ." You say you have trouble deciding? Work out more than one. You say the kind of job you had was so routine that there was no opportunity for achievement? Or that you just did your job— nothing special about it? Or that you're no writer? Not to worry. Here's a simple outline that will help you to uncover the real you—the person with the skills to make a productive addition to the organization that would be smart enough to hire you:

As a (your job title) _____
I was
    responsible for _____
    in charge of _____
    asked to solve the problem of _____
    given the assignment of _____
    worked with ____ in order to _____
    worked for ____ with the responsibility to _____

To achieve the desired result, I
    designed a _____
    organized a series of experiments that _____
    managed a team of _____
    developed a system for _____
    created a method of _____
    had to learn _____
    established a procedure that _____

Here's how my (method, system, experiment, procedure) worked:

What I did first: (Drew up a plan, wrote specifications,

conducted research, planned a budget, established a time frame, organized a team)

What I did next: (Built a model, tested various approaches, established assignments, monitored results) What next, and so on . . .

Here are some of the problems encountered, and how I helped to solve them:

Problem—solution

Here are the results:
(Production/efficiency) was improved by _____
(Man-hours/costs) were reduced by _____
Error factors went down by _____
(Income/profit) was increased by _____

At first glance, this may look like the outline you got from your camp counselor to encourage writing letters home. Well, what was wrong with that if it helped you to write your first letter? And the chances are very good that this is the first time you've ever written about one of your major achievements. You may have created your share of resumes with those vague one-liners that described your *experience*, but this is different. This is a detailed account of your most important achievement.

You're not writing the story of your working life. That might take volumes. Instead, try 200 Words or so—this will be the WORD BANK you can draw upon to help you develop more effective letters, resumes, and ways of presenting your abilities during the interview itself.

Here is a completed example:

As a Data Manager, I was in charge of developing systems for reporting and evaluating performance data from twenty-four regional offices. These data had been submitted on a monthly basis, which meant that vital information could be as much as thirty days old. **I was asked to solve the problem of** getting more timely and accurate data from twenty-four regional management teams that were already "too busy." I established an objective of having an accurate report from each office communicated every Monday.

To achieve the desired result, I first developed a communication procedure to track the distribution of each element of the data. I determined who was using these data and how. My research with branch management showed that almost a third of the data came into use only at the end of a quarter. I was able to design a modification of several data fields, which simplified reporting by eliminating almost twenty percent of the present entries.

Despite the preparation of a manual that taught the simpler and more efficient reporting system, **the major problem I encountered** was in achieving my goal of a weekly report. To motivate cooperation, I developed an incentive program of a weekend at some resort hotel within the region.

As a result, the data system revisions and incentive program worked together to generate a weekly data flow that, according to management, helped to improve productivity by twenty-five percent. The error factor fell to less than five percent. The incentive paid for itself many times over.

To design the data gathering, analysis, and reporting program I had to master the DEC VAX/ULTRIX operating system, the db-VISTA database package, and db-QUERY language to run reports.

It's a little more than 200 Words, but that's OK. It's not too long. And it's a clear and straightforward account of a clear and straightforward achievement. It explains the what, why, and how. Notice that it carefully omits the where. This maximizes your range of possibilities by organizing your achievements so that they apply to a number of different fields.

For example, can you identify the industry in which this achievement was accomplished? Was it banking, trucking, manufacturing and distribution, market research, retailing, insurance, travel, social services, auto rental, construction, securities, real estate, fuel delivery, or whatever else you can think of? By placing the focus on your major achievement and the skills it took to produce it instead of on the environment in which it was achieved, you give yourself more options.

To see how this works for you, go back over your own 200 Words and make a list of the skills represented. Then compare it to the one on the following page. Don't cheat.

How many did you come up with? Just highlighting the appropriate phrases creates a pretty good answer to the question, "Why me?" Because you are a:

• Developer of systems
• Reporter and evaluator of performance data
• Problem solver
• Developer of procedures
• Conductor of research
• Simplifier of reporting systems

What's more, you are able to:

• Master complex data systems
• Communicate with branch management
• Prepare manuals
• Teach and train
• Motivate

- Develop incentive programs
- Set and achieve objectives

Most important, your work delivers results:

- Productivity improved by twenty-five percent
- Error factor reduced to less than five percent

Now here's a funny thing. Past experience has shown that whether butcher, baker, candlestick maker, almost without exception, you will have one of three basic responses to the idea of beginning the Job-Getting Process with a 200-Word account of your most important achievement. Which of them is in your mind right now? The truth, remember:

1) I'm one of those people who needs a job sooner than right away. This Process sounds too much like beginning at the beginning. I want to start toward the end in order to save time.

2) I have plenty of important achievements in my work record. I don't need this warm-up exercise. Just give me the ball, put me on the mound, and let me pitch. I'll sell myself during the interview.

3) I have no achievements. My job was routine. I was a (draftsman) (administrative assistant) (bookkeeper) who simply carried out the functions designed by others.

Notice how none of the three sounds anything like "This looks as if it might work so let me get started"? That's OK. If you'd rather put another batch of resumes in the mail, do that. But leave a bookmark at this spot. Experience has shown that you'll be back.

If you're in a hurry (Response #1), there's no way to dissuade you from listing your entire background on a sheet of paper and rushing 100 copies to whomever it might concern. That kind of Buck-Shot Resume is the principal cliché of the job-hunting world. Not because it works so well. Its efficiency as an interview-generator ranges from 2%–5%, depending on whom you're willing to believe. But up till now it's been the only game in town. It has, in fact, become part of the language:

- "Look, we have no openings right now, but send me your resume."
- "Do not telephone. Send resume and salary requirements to . . ."
- "I'm sorry, but the Decision-Maker is too busy to see you right now. Why not leave your resume and he/she will be in touch with you."

Why then has the Buck-Shot Resume survived this long? Because it's easy. It's easy on you because you prepare a one-sheet menu of your work history. Now you have something to send, leave, and pass around to people who want to end the communication and know that asking for it will get rid of you. During good times when there are plenty of job opportunities, Decision-Makers are less inclined to round-file them. But what happens when times are tough and the job-search is more competitive? What happens when there is more talent in the woodwork than there are openings? Then the Buck-Shot Resume makes it easy on the Decision-Maker to dispose of when there is no opening. It also makes it easy for the Decision-Maker to dispose of you when there is an opening. All that's needed is an Inside-Track resume in that same pile of mail prepared by someone who has taken the time and trouble to get on the Inside Track. Once the Decision-Maker compares the Inside-Track Resume with your Buck-Shot effort, one of those "Thank you for your interest but other applicants had better qualifications" letters is practically in the mail to you.

But if you're determined to go the standard resume route, get it over with. You'll feel better. Whoever helps you to prepare it will feel better. And more to the point, you'll have an acceptable answer to the annoying question you're likely to overhear at your local watering hole these days:

PERSON #1: *How's the job-hunt going?*
PERSON #2: *I sent out one hundred resumes.*
PERSON #1: *And?*
PERSON #2: *I'll tell you in a minute. Bartender, a Perrier and lime, please. I have an interview in an hour.*
PERSON #1: *Hey, great! Here's luck.*
PERSON #2: *Save the luck. It's with a headhunter. I sent out a hundred resumes to banks and personnel agencies specializing in banking and got twenty answers.*
PERSON #1: *Fantastic! That's a twenty percent response.*
PERSON #2: *Thanks, but after eleven years in banking, I could have arrived at those figures on my own. To tell the truth, the numbers are misleading. What I got was twelve promises from personnel departments to keep my resume on file, three agencies who invited me to come in for an interview though they had nothing suitable at the moment, and one job possibility at a branch in Nowheresville that isn't even in my specialty.*
PERSON #1: *Forgive the observation, but that's only sixteen.*
PERSON #2: *I left out the four that told me banking was off right now and they're not hiring. That's also in the category of information I really didn't need. Maybe I will have a drink after all. Bartender!*

There's no saying that a Buck-Shot resume can't connect. But if you're really in a hurry to get a job, it's a pretty passive way to pursue your objective. What you're doing is firing a shotgun with your eyes closed and hoping a pellet will hit, when what these times and your personal situation call for is a carefully aimed campaign directed where it will do the most good. So send out the resumes if you feel you absolutely, positively must. But then, don't wait to hear. Waiting wastes time, and time is what you don't have. Instead, let's get to work.

If you could write a book about your many achievements (Response #2) and look forward to telling some unsuspecting Decision-Maker "all about yourself," with the accent on the "all," get ready to answer one question: How are you going to get the interview in the first place? If you don't happen to be rich in the kind of Contacts that can set up any number of opportunities to pitch yourself, what then? And even if you are, which of your many achievements would do the best job of getting the job?

You could experiment. But using the trial-and-error approach with good Contacts is like setting fire to your unemployment check. It may give you a temporary, warm feeling, but it makes it hard to cash.

This doesn't mean there's no advantage to having more than one achievement. On the contrary. The more the better. Compiling a dossier of these achievements and then targeting each of them at the most likely job opportunity reduces the risk of error and the loss of yet another valuable contact.

Relative anonymity (Response #3) sounds limiting, but if you have any positive work experience at all, it means that you convinced someone that you were good enough to hire. If you stayed with the job, it means your work was good enough to keep you hired. If your responsibilities were increased and your salary went up as well, it means you were good enough to promote.

You could save most of the 200 Words by simply writing, "I was good." Or you could expand the message by writing what you were good at.

Was your work repetitious? Under ordinary circumstances, this might lead to boredom, which leads to costly errors, tardiness, sick days, and an addiction to water-cooler gossip. But you found a way of making the job more interesting. How? What approach did you use? What skills did it bring into play? What was the result?

Or were you given a job for which you had to learn a special skill or two? Not only were you successful at learning the skill, but you did so in record time. People who are eager to learn new skills in order to take on new responsibility make the best kind of people to hire.

Write it down. Polish it until, like the sample, it reflects a dozen skills you weren't even aware you had until you focused on them.

How to research the fields or organizations you have targeted

Here's the key question: How well do your skills match those required by the job, field, or organization you've targeted?

Actually, that's not true. The key question *really* is: What skills are required by the job, field, or organization you've targeted?

If the two questions sound the same to you, your job-getting could be in serious trouble. The first puts the focus on how well you measure up. If you're not feeling too positive about yourself, that could be pretty depressing. The second question, on the other hand, puts the focus on the requirements. That's where it belongs. Once you've stopped measuring yourself, you can start measuring them.

For example, suppose you were the data manager who wrote the 200 Words outlining your most important achievement back on page 35. Your previous field was banking. Now you'd like to avoid the risk of yet another down-sizing by looking into other fields where your skills might be put to even better use. You were thinking of the kind of working environment where your individual productivity would have a specific impact on the bottom line. The philosophy is basic. The closer you are to the profitability of the organization, the stronger your hold on your job and on your personal growth in terms of money and power.

This is no plug for *The Wall Street Journal, Crain's, Business Week*, the business section of a big-city newspaper, or any other business publication, but reading them would give you a pretty good picture of which firms are stepping out while others are marking time.

Whoops! Here's an article about the growth of the aftermarket auto parts business. What it means in English is that some aggressive marketer is taking advantage of the downturn in new car sales by providing the parts to fix the old ones. Hundreds of franchised outlets are doing the sales and installation, monitored by regional offices from coast to coast.

What it means in computereze is data. Lots of data. Inventory control data. Sales and performance data. Personnel data. Market potential data.

What it means in terms of management is the need to motivate the reporting of timely, accurate data so that it can be analyzed and exploited for maximum profitability.

Oh, you say you already had that idea? And you did what? I'm sorry, the noise in this bar is so loud I can't hear you. Say it again. You looked up the address of the company and sent them your resume. Aha. And you got a letter from their personnel department saying there were no openings at this time? How surprising! You sent an unrequested resume that featured your banking experience to nobody in particular at an auto parts company, and you got nada. Which means the whole idea stinks, right? That's what I thought. Bartender, make it a double!

It's no accident that the first of the three R's is Research.

What you know about your Target field or organization is the pivot on which your career might spin off in a new direction. And you can learn a great deal with just one question:

By what criteria are people hired for the kind of job you're looking for in the field or organization you've targeted?

Then it's just a matter of deciding which of those criteria you can meet and which you can't. Are there too many can't-do's? What courses, training, practice sessions, or period of apprenticeship would help you to learn them?

Wait. Before you say the job you're after has the same criteria no matter where you go and you already know them and can therefore skip the Research, pay careful attention to the next three statements:

- You could be right.
- You could be wrong.
- Either way, you're wrong.

Even if you're absolutely 100% sure you have all the information you need, the very act of asking for it does something nothing else can do. It switches you from the outside to the inside track:

- You'll be making or meeting Contacts in the Target field or organization, which is particularly important if it's new to you.
- You'll be up-dating your information, which is particularly important if you haven't been job-hunting in a while.
- You'll be taking action rather than depending on ads or agencies, which is particularly important when you need a Feeling of Activity.
- You'll be able to make a more accurate decision about how happy you'll be in that field or organization, which is

particularly important if you're the kind of person who likes to be happy.

Make Contacts who can help you get on the Inside Track

You may already have some Contacts who are in the Target field or organization you're researching. You'll want more. You may not have some Contacts in the Target field or organization you're researching. You'll want to make some. But before you start, write this message to yourself on your bathroom mirror in shaving cream or lipstick:

"What I'm after is a job. But during the Research phase of the Process, what I'm after is information."

Before you say that you're already trying this approach and getting nowhere, let me order another drink. Bartender! Oops—forget it for now. He's trapped by the lament of the guy on the next stool:

> GUY: *I've been sitting here an hour and I don't think he's going to show. Some friend, right? First it takes me three or four phone calls to reach him, and then he stands me up. It's been that way ever since I've been out on the street— people treating me like unemployment is contagious. There has to be one of them who can steer me to a job. But it's always the same deal. Send me your resume. So I do. Then I call and call and all I get is that suspicious pause while somebody "checks to see if he's in" and finds he's not. Well, to hell with it. And to hell with him. I'll have another.*

If you're drowning that kind of sorrow, or drowning in it— take heart. Even during good times, dropping out of the loop of the feverishly employed will isolate you from those who still have deadlines to meet. And bad times? Unless you count among your acquaintances those whose souls are ready for beatification, you're on your own. If you expect job leads but your Contacts have no job leads for you—and during bad times that's not unusual—what's the point of spending time with you? There isn't any, is there?

Yes, there is. As long as:

- You're a person worth talking to because you have something of value to offer to somebody—as proven by your 200 Words.
- You've expanded your horizons by targeting a range of industries and organizations that could make good use of what you have to offer.
- You really believe that sign on your bathroom mirror and are prepared to live up to it. Repeat it after me:

"What I'm after is a job. But during the Research phase of the Process, what I'm after is information."

So start over. Make a list of the people you know who can give you the information you need—even if they've brushed you off before. Then make a list of the people you know who know someone who can give you the information you need—even if they've brushed you off before.

STEP 2

Learn How to Use Your WORD BANK to Create the Kind of **SELF-PRESENTATION** That Will Initiate Professional Discussions with People Who Can Help You Match Your Skills to the Criteria of the Job You Want

There is a caveat like a Surgeon General's warning in the margin of this section. You may not be able to see it, but it's there. It tells you that the whole idea of networking has been given a bad name and that there is a general mistrust of information-seekers. Small wonder. Many a Decision-Maker, out of the kindness of his or her heart, has agreed to spend time with someone supposedly looking for information only to come face-to-face with someone pleading for a job that wasn't there.

WARNING: Your SELF-PRESENTATION had better be good—and it (and you) had better be honest.

MAKING CONTACTS IN YOUR TARGET FIRMS OR INDUSTRIES

For some reason it seems to be perfectly OK to answer ads that call for your specialty in firms or industries that are outside your area of experience, but not OK to deliberately seek them out. Why not? Is it the effort that's involved? It is easier to be passive than active. Is it fear of rejection? You may run into some criteria you can't meet, but these collisions are rarely fatal. Or is it simply lack of imagination? That's the easiest hurdle to get over. Thirty minutes with an industrial directory will give you all the possibilities you need. So make a list.

How to research your target firms or industries

Every business is different. While there are some common denominators that apply to broad categories of enterprise—profit vs. non-profit, manufacturing vs. distributing, commercial vs. academic—every business *is* different. There are differences in trade language, customs, and the structure of the decision-making ladder. A good rule of thumb when conducting your research is to try like crazy to resist preconceived notions and behave like what you are—a foreigner. Instead of guide books, dictionaries, and a few restaurant recommendations, you'll need company literature, articles in the business press or trade journals, and some recommendations of whom to see.

Let's suppose, like the data person you met in Step 1, you're fascinated by the opportunities that may exist in the auto aftermarket industry. Fortunately, every industry worthy of the name has a trade press. Maybe it's not the greatest leisure-reading experience of your life, but it will give you an insight into the customs and language of the business:

- What do they call the people who buy from them? Customers, Franchisees, Dealers, Owners, Independent Operators, Retailers, Distributors, Installers, Service Outlets?
- Through whom do they deal with their customers? Direct, Distributors, Factory Reps, Area Managers, Regional Warehouse Sales Staff?
- How do they communicate with their customers? Catalogues, Specification Books, Service Manuals, Price Lists, Computer Networks, Trade Shows, Sales Meetings, Personal Reps?
- How's business? Expanding because of current market opportunities? Hurting, because of costly administrative problems? Surviving, despite severe competition? Losing ground to . . . ?

While a few more questions may occur to you, keep in mind that you don't have to learn everything there is to know. This would not only be a bit difficult to accomplish from the outside but might lead you into the little-knowledge-is-dangerous minefield. All you really have to know going in is enough language and custom to understand what you're being told.

How to draw on your WORD BANK to create effective CONTACT LETTERS

The CONTACT LETTER reflects the message on your bathroom mirror. It announces your need for information.

Let's say you know someone in the field you've targeted. In fact, you know him or her well enough to just ring up. But don't touch that dial. Instead, take a piece of that stationery you bought and write:

Mr. John Contact
Exact Title
World Technologies
123 Universe Ave.
Any City, U.S.A.

Dear John,

As you may have heard, the down-sizing at Amalgamated Bank and Trust requires that I make a new start. Ideally, this would be with the kind of organization that could make best use of the kind of results I've achieved in data management.

For example, one assignment made me responsible for getting more timely and accurate data from twenty-four regional management teams that were already "too busy." My first step was to develop a communication procedure to track the distribution of each element of the data to determine who was using it and why. Research with branch management enabled me to simplify reporting by eliminating almost twenty percent of the present entries. The end result was a weekly data flow that, according to management, helped to

CREATING A SELF-PRESENTATION 51

improve productivity by twenty-five percent. The error factor fell to less than five percent.

To design the data gathering, analysis, and reporting program I had to master the DEC VAX/ULTRIX operating system, the db-VISTA database package, and db-QUERY language to run reports.

Right now I'm in the process of exploring several career alternatives. My initial research has shown that the aftermarket industry has a particular need for the kind of timely, accurate data flow that I can achieve. But before I make any decisions, I'm trying to benefit from the counsel of people like you who really know the industry from the inside.

Could we meet long enough for me to ask just one question, make some notes, and be on my way?

If it's okay, I'll call you first thing on Thursday to set a time. If that's not convenient, will you leave word with your secretary about the best time to get together?

Thanks John, I appreciate it.

(Signed)

This entire letter, from beginning to end, is nothing but a simple, honest request for information. Each word says exactly what it means:

As you may have heard, the down-sizing at Amalgamated Bank and Trust requires that I make a new start.

Well, that's what happened to your previous job. You didn't resign to explore new opportunities. The bank scaled back and you were cut. But this is the only reference to the environment in which you did your job. If this Contact is your friend, he or she would know that anyway. From then on you focus on your achievement and how it would apply to the field you've targeted.

Even if you've targeted another bank department in another specialty, the term "new start" suggests that you're open to a broader range of possibilities than your previous job, title, or level of authority might indicate. You're out to broaden that range of possibilities, remember?

Ideally, this would be with the kind of organization that could make best use of the kind of results I've achieved in data management.

The people who cut me made one hell of a mistake, because I'm the kind of person who gets results. But their loss is somebody else's gain.

For example, one assignment made me responsible for getting more timely and accurate data from twenty-four regional management teams that were already "too busy." My first step was to develop a communication procedure to track the distribution of each element of the data to determine who was using it and why. Research with branch management enabled me to simplify reporting by eliminating almost twenty percent of the present entries. The end result was a weekly data flow that, according to management, helped to improve productivity by twenty-five percent. The error factor fell to less than five percent.

To design the data gathering, analysis, and reporting program I had to master the DEC VAX/ULTRIX operating system, the db-VISTA database package, and db-QUERY language to run reports.

Recognize the last two paragraphs? Each word came right out of the WORD BANK you created with your 200 Words. What it says is what you did. It also says that you're no loser who should be put off with excuses about trips out of town. It says that you're someone worth helping because you're in a position to be of help to someone in an organization looking for more productive data management. And that was only one assignment. You could offer others. But not right now. Now what you want is to get information, not give it.

Right now I'm in the process of exploring several career alternatives.

Once again, that's exactly what you're doing. And you're doing it pretty well, because you've done some homework on your own.

My initial research has shown that the aftermarket industry has a particular need for the kind of timely, accurate data flow that I can achieve.

Now, how did you know that? Did you go to the business shelves of your library and research the field? Did you read the trade magazines and professional journals? Did you make copies of those pieces of information that pertained to you and your situation? Best use of a library card that was ever invented.

But before I make any decisions, I'm trying to benefit from the counsel of people like you who really know the industry from the inside.

What's this? You're not asking your good friend and buddy for a job? That's just as well. Asking for a job that isn't there will generally get you the "out of town" response. But if by some chance—some long chance—there is an opening, you'll hear about it during your meeting.

Could we meet long enough for me to ask just one question, make some notes, and be on my way?

What's the one question? If you want to know by what criteria people in your specialty are hired in the field of after-market auto parts, that's it. Isn't it easy when you say just what you mean?

If it's okay, I'll call you first thing on Thursday to set a time. If that's not convenient, will you leave word with your secretary about the best time to get together?

You've stressed the fact that it's information you're looking for this time around—which is why it's OK to recontact people who may have already brushed you off. You've outlined some specific skills that make you a good person to see—which is why it's OK to recontact people who may have already brushed you off. And you've promised to ask just one question, make some notes, and be on your way—which means a concise and goal-oriented conversation instead of a job plea. So you won't need a lot of time.

Thanks John, I appreciate it.

And you do.

Asking people for information appeals to their status, their expertise, their sense of their own security. Asking people for a job appeals to their sympathy, empathy, and generosity. Stick with the first appeal. You're less likely to be disappointed.

How do you explain what you're after? How do you make clear what it is you want? Here we're on dangerous ground because this sample letter suggests specific words. Not tricky words. Not words you haven't heard before. Not words you haven't used before. But maybe words you would not choose to use in this particular combination in this particular situation.

It's more than understanding the difference between these two statements:

"I'm looking for a job in this industry and I wonder if you can help me."

"I'm looking for information about this industry and I understand you're an expert."

Experience has shown that there's no sense in saying that experience has shown certain words and phrases are more effective than others. If you have such an ego-resistance to the idea of someone else "putting words in your mouth" that "don't sound like you," think again. Haven't you ever:

• Repeated a funny story someone told you?.
• Said a prayer you found in some religious text?
• Acted in a play someone else wrote?
• Quoted some famous figure to make a point?
• Used a fact or figure you learned at school?

If you have a problem using words and ideas other than your own, we're on a collision course. Because you're going to get nothing but specific examples of what has proven to be clear, honest, effective, persuasive communication. If you want to change the letter so it sounds "more like you," go ahead. Just remember that you're on this page because what sounded like you hasn't worked. Make sure your CONTACT LETTER says what the example says.

And keep it simple. A simple letter with straightforward wording is the hardest to write—which is why so many people hate letters and prefer to just pick up the phone. In fact, why not just pick up the phone and give John a call? There are at least three reasons:

The first reason is timing. Imagine that your Contact is waiting for a call from a major customer, his boss, the hospital, his lawyer, his lover, or the doctor who performed those special tests just that morning. In other words, there is more going on between the ears of the person you're trying to reach, Horatio, than you can anticipate. Your call at the wrong time is an invasion.

The second reason is one of communication. A phone call out of the blue can never come across as clearly as a well-planned letter. You might wind up sounding like you're asking for a job—which you're not. And he may not have one to give you. Bingo! There goes the Contact.

It's also important to remember that you're asking for a favor. True, you have skills and experience that might repay that favor many times over. But that's in the future. This is now, when he's busy, when he "really doesn't have any place for you."

The third reason is one of simple courtesy. While your Contact may have all the time in the world to see you, chances are better than even money that some times are better than others. A letter rather than an untimely phone call gives your Contact the chance to plan the time.

Most important, your Contact may want to do some research on your behalf. He may even want to contact other Contacts on your behalf. He may even want to pass your letter around! This too, will take time.

Does this mean that the CONTACT LETTER is an automatic door-opener? No. But at the very least it sets up a more productive phone call. And the better the letter, the more productive the call.

It's at this point that the first droplet of pessimism stains your pad. Up till now, your 200 Words and the skills they represented were making you feel pretty good about yourself. You had even made a list of a number of Target industries or organizations where your know-how would be of great value. You even verified your potential with some trips to the library, where the business directories and trade publications helped you bring your Target into closer focus. But then you think the CONTACT LETTER won't work for you *because*:

- You have no Contacts in your Target industry or organization.
- You don't feel comfortable meeting people to whom you have not been introduced.
- You're no good at writing letters.

Welcome to your first crossroad, stranger. Certainly, making a Contact in this anti-contact society is no easy job. After all, this is the era of the Walkman, where we move around with our ears plugged against hearing each other, our eyes averted from sights that might be unpleasant, and engage in tribal dances created so that we can feel connected without even touching. How, in the face of this negative atmosphere, made even more negative by that mythic monster, the economy, can you hope to get the CONTACT LETTER to work for you? *Unless . . .*

- You learn how to make a specific contact in your Target industry or organization.
- You learn how to feel comfortable meeting someone to whom you have not been introduced.
- You learn how to write a focused letter that works.

Note the change from pessimism to optimism? By swapping the word "unless" for the licked-before-you-start "because," you at least establish the possibility of success—if you can just learn a few specific job-getting skills. This doesn't mean you have to "learn to make contacts." That's much too big an ambition for your time frame. As is learning to feel comfortable meeting strangers, or writing letters, if that hasn't been your life pattern.

Instead, change one habit. Rather than wasting your precious time with popular magazines, focus your reading on your Target organization or industry. Make note of the names in the articles. Make note of the quotes. And if an article is authored by some authority in the business, all the better. Now your CONTACT LETTER reads:

Dear Contact-You-Don't-Know-But-Read-About,

Your article, "Merchandising Auto Parts for the Upscale Market" in the June issue of *Aftermarket Magazine* was very informative. But since my expertise is data management, not aftermarket, it got me to wondering. How does your industry gather and monitor the data needed to make the "corrections upward or downward" that you referred to?

My reason for asking is that after eleven years in data management, I'm looking for a new start in a dynamic business environment. Ideally, this would be with an organization that could make best use of the kind of results I've achieved in gathering and analyzing data.

By now you know the drill. The Contact may be flattered by your interest or intrigued by the tone of your letter. The question, however, still remains: Why should he/she give you the time of day? An excerpt from your 200 Words should answer that question.

Then, since the Contact is not a friend or a friend of a friend, you might wish to alter the last paragraph as follows:

If it's OK, I'll call you first thing on Thursday to set a time. If that's not convenient, will you leave word with your secretary about the best time to talk?
Thanks, Mr. (Ms.)_____. I appreciate it.

The introductory paragraph and the last sentence are different, but this is the same CONTACT LETTER you would write to someone you know in the business. Once again, it's nothing but a simple, honest request for information, and, as in the previous example, each word says exactly what it means:

Your article, "Merchandising Auto Parts for the Upscale Market" in the June issue of Aftermarket Magazine *was very informative.*

It may not be an article. It may be just a quote. It may be a reference to the person you're writing. Whatever the case, the term "informative" doesn't fawn. It simply states the truth about your reaction to what you read. It also shows that you believe in researching before you make a contact.

But since my expertise is data management, not aftermarket, it got me to wondering. How does your industry gather and monitor the data needed to make the "corrections upward or downward" that you referred to?

Finding a specific reference is what good research is all about. Quoting it is even better. And, as you will find, good research leads to more research. How *does* the aftermarket industry in general or this organization in particular gather and monitor its data? After all, your expertise is data management, not aftermarket, so it's a logical question for you to ask.

My reason for asking is that after eleven years in data management, I'm looking for a new start in a dynamic business environment. Ideally, this would be with an organization that could make best use of the kind of results I've achieved in gathering and analyzing data.

Once again, are you looking for a job? NO! Are you looking for information? YES! And the rest of the letter is the same as before.

Nothing fancy. You don't have to learn to make contacts, you've just made one. When you meet, your CONTACT LETTER will have introduced you. You'll even have a topic of conversation already established.

Of course there's always the possibility that your target doesn't go in for trade publicity—or publicity of any kind, for that matter. So let's make it hard. How do you research an organization that doesn't talk about itself?

The happy fact is that practically everyone does, in one form or another:

- In an Annual Report, which you can get by asking for one or asking someone in the business to ask for one, or by going to the head office if it's within range.
- Product literature, which you can get in the same way.
- Professional Conferences in which your target participates. Attending can get you the information you need and a lot more in the way of actual handshakes.

All that changes is the first paragraph of your CONTACT LETTER. Everything else remains exactly the same:

Dear Contact-You-Don't-Know-But-Read-About,

Your most recent Annual Report on your position in the aftermarket industry was very informative. I made particular note of your organization's plan to merchandise more aggressively in the upscale market. But since my expertise is data management, not aftermarket, it got me to wondering. How does your industry gather and monitor the data needed to track the upscale market and measure your penetration?

My reason for asking is . . . etc.

If you don't know anyone, or you don't know anyone who knows anyone, or have never read anything by or about anyone, just call the organizations you've targeted and ask for the names and titles of the Decision-Makers.

THEY: *Good morning, Aftermarket Industries.*

YOU: *Good morning. This is (your name) and I'm writing a letter to the head of your data department. Could you please tell me his or her name?*

THEY: *That would be Claire Good-Kind*

YOU: *Is that C-L-A-I-R . . . ?*

THEY: *With an E at the end. And the last name is hyphenated. G-O-O-D hyphen K-I-N-D.*

YOU: *Thanks very much. What is Mrs. Good-Kind's title, by the way?*

THEY: *Director, MIS Department.*

YOU: *You've been very courteous and I'd like to tell that to Ms. Good-kind. May I ask your name?*

Why all this detail about the simple procedure of getting or verifying a name? Not everybody is as friendly and cooperative as in this example. There was a time when organizations were very sensitive to the way in which their contact employees responded to the public. Many companies felt—and rightly so—that every caller was a potential customer and should be treated accordingly. But good manners have given way to efficiency. Now you're lucky to get a live person instead of a toneless, there's-nobody-here-but-us-recordings voice that tells you what button to push. And luckier still if the live person isn't getting ten calls a minute or has a personnel guide handy.

The last thing you want to do is send a personal letter to someone whose name, gender, and title are inaccurate. That's a fast goodbye! So before you get ready to say "Hello," get your script ready and practice your best telephone voice:

1) Introduce yourself. A busy operator is less likely to hang up on someone whose name they have just learned.

2) Start spelling the name you have just heard immediately, instead of saying your thanks. To a busy operator, "thank you" is the same as "goodbye."

3) Work from a script so that in case you are put on hold you can pick up at the right spot.

4) Work from a script so your conversation isn't slowed with "a-a-ahs." Respect the fact that the operator owes you nothing.

5) Work from a script so that you'll remember to compliment a helpful operator.

6) Work from a script so that in case the operator is unable to give you the information you need, you'll be ready to ask to be transferred to the data department and start the script over again—with variations:

THEY: *Data Department. Irene Daily.*
YOU: *Good morning, Ms. Daily. This is (your name) and I'm writing a letter to the head of your data department. Could you please tell me his or her name?*
THEY: *That would be Claire Good-Kind*
YOU: *Is that C-L-A-I-R . . . ?*
THEY: *With an E at the end. And her last name is hyphenated. G-O-O-D hyphen K-I-N-D.*
YOU: *Thanks very much. What is Ms. Good-Kind's title, by the way?*
THEY: *Director, MIS Department.*

YOU: *You've been very courteous, Ms. Daily, and I'll tell that to Ms. Good-Kind. Thanks again.*

How to call them because they won't call you

Well, here it is—first thing Thursday morning. There's the phone. There's the number. There's the name. And there's that funny but familiar feeling in the pit of your stomach that things will not go well. You don't know this person. You've already made a number of phone calls and sent a number of resumes. And you're reading this book because they didn't work. Why should the results of this effort be any different?

Instead of cold-calling friends hoping that one of them can steer you to a job, you are using your major achievements to contact people you know or people you have researched to ask them for the information you need in order to create an Inside-Track Resume.

Instead of limiting yourself to your experience in a particular environment, you're focusing on your major achievements and the skills that can be applied to a number of Target businesses or industries.

Instead of trusting luck and your fantastic ability to say just the right thing at the right time, you rehearse your Thursday morning call in terms of the following possibilities:

- Your Contact has read your letter, is willing to provide the information you need, and is ready to set up an appointment.
- Your Contact has read your letter, is willing to provide the information you need, but is too busy to set up an appointment right now.

- Your Contact has read your letter but feels he or she is the wrong person to give you the information you need.
- Your Contact has read your letter, does not wish to get involved, and wants to dispose of you as quickly as possible.
- Your Contact has not read your letter and does not remember receiving it.

This might be a great time to check on whether you're an optimist or a pessimist. Of those five basic possibilities how many are positive and how many are negative? Only the first seems positive, *unless* you're prepared to deal with each situation before you make the follow-up call. In that case, anything could be positive.

Consider for a moment the number of people—yourself included—who may have asked these same Contacts to help them locate a job. Consider the number of people—yourself included—who may have pretended to be asking these same Contacts for information but wound up asking for a job. If they have no jobs to offer, this past experience is going to make some of those Contacts gun-shy enough to want to avoid involvement in your needs.

It isn't fair. Most of us, at one time or another, have encountered a mentor who played a vital role in our lives. Maybe it was a teacher, a colleague, a boss whose help was accepted. You would think that, based on the principle that help accepted is an obligation to pass it on, we would all be more supportive of one another. But who said it would be that way? So prepare.

THEY: *Data Department. Irene Daily.*
YOU: *Good morning, Ms. Daily. Nice to talk to you again. This is (your name). I told Claire Good-Kind that I would call her this morning about the best time for an appointment.*
THEY: *Oh, yes (your name.) She has you in her book for two*

possibilities: Friday, the 9th, at 2:00, or Monday, the 12th at 11.

YOU: *The Friday date sounds good. I look forward to seeing you. By the way, is there any special floor or office I should ask for?*

THEY: *We're on seven.*

YOU: *Great! Thanks a lot, Ms. Daily. I'll see you on Friday, the 9th, at 2:00.*

Clear, straightforward communication doesn't need an explanation of the why's and wherefore's. Just count the goodies:

- The nice thing about remembering the names of the people you talk to—and making clear that you remember them—is just that. It's nice.
- Referring to your contact by first and last name is friendlier than the Mr., Mrs., or Ms.
- Short and to the point is good too. You promised to call and here you are.
- Your CONTACT LETTER requesting information rather than a Buck-Shot Resume asking for a job was a professional approach that generated interest on the part of a fellow professional. Maybe it's your achievement she wants to talk about. Maybe she's the kind of person who likes to help other people. Either way, it's good for you.
- The way she handled the appointment indicates that Claire Good-Kind is efficient and well-organized. Make sure you are when you come to call.
- Picking the earlier date is a good move. You've got a backup just in case.

Sounds hard to believe, does it? It all depends on how effective your 200 Words are. If you didn't spend much time on them, why should anyone else? But even the most interesting achievement might fall on busy ears. What if the contact is interested enough to come to the phone but too busy to see you right now? Frustrating, isn't it? Don't get angry. Get ready. You're going to hear one of two directives:

Call again on Monday.

This is code for a possible time crunch during the week ahead. Ms. Good-Kind doesn't want to get locked in to a commitment she can't keep because she's too nice a person to make a date and then stand you up. That speaks well for her.

Speaking for yourself, you'll need only twenty minutes. And if it's not an out-of-town trip, you're willing to come to her office and wait for an opening, aren't you? And if there is any industry literature she could leave for you to study while you're waiting, that would be a real help. Is there any morning or afternoon that offers the best chance?

So speak for yourself:

YOU: *It sounds like there could be a possible time crunch during the week ahead, Ms. Good-Kind, and that you're too nice a person to make a date you might not be able to keep. I really appreciate that. But, I need only twenty minutes—and I'm more than willing to come to your office and wait for an opening. No obligation. And if there is any industry literature you could leave for me to study while I'm waiting, that would be a real help all in itself. Is there any morning or afternoon that offers the best chance?*

How easy it is to communicate simply and directly when you take the time and trouble to understand what the other person may be thinking. *May* be thinking, mind you. This is not an absolute science. But anticipating your Contact's position and being prepared can help you to avoid that dangerous, fast-talking, high-volume speech pattern that sounds like pressure when it's really just panic.

Incidentally, if you're getting this information from a secretary or assistant, the same response applies.

The second possibility is: Call me sometime later in the month.

In the technical language of communication, this is called an oh-oh. Your Contact is interested enough to see you but not willing to set aside a major project, divorce proceeding, business trip, elective surgery, or vacation. The problem is the same as in the previous situation. You only want twenty minutes, but, for your Contact, clearing the mind can be as difficult as clearing the calendar.

YOU: *It sounds like there could be a possible time crunch during the weeks ahead, Ms. Good-Kind, and that you're too nice a person to make a date you may not be able to keep. I really appreciate that. Would contacting you on the 21st be a better time? Or would the 28th be even better?*
THEY: *The 28th, I think.*
YOU: *Great! Would you have any industry literature I might study in the meantime? If you could leave it for me with someone I'll be happy to come by tomorrow and pick it up. I would be most grateful, and then whatever time you can spare me when we meet will be far more productive.*

Ask yourself: How different is this from making a date with a friend? Not everybody runs on the same timetable. Many social and business meetings are a matter of negotiating the best time for all concerned. But if you're anxious—and your anxiety shows—it could make people nervous. It could make *you* nervous. Instead of sounding like a competent professional looking for information from a fellow professional, you sound like a job-seeker grasping at opportunity. So in addition to getting ready for any response, you might even want to rehearse. Here are some tips from people who have been there:

- Watch your word rate. Talking fast so that people won't hang up on you generally has the opposite effect. The more relaxed you sound, the more relaxed they'll be.
- Watch your volume. Try not to sound any louder than the voice you're listening to. Otherwise, your conversation could take on the tone of an attack.
- Watch your temper. Remember, it's a favor you're after, not an argument. Take deep breaths.
- And never, never, never, never interrupt. The reasons are too obvious to take any time for.

How to persuade people who won't give you the time of day

Your Contact read your letter and was interested—but feels he or she is the wrong person to give you the information you need.

> YOU: *It was good of you to take the time to read my letter, Ms. Good-Kind. And I appreciate your frankness. As my letter explained, I'm looking for information about the criteria by which people with my skills in data gathering would be hired in your industry. Does that idea suggest anyone else you know who might be able to give me the information I need? I'd be most grateful for your help— and would not use your name without your permission.*

People who would like to help you but don't know how often know others who do. They may even volunteer the names. Or you may have to ask. Either way, it's good manners—and good sense—to promise not to use their name without permission. (Unless they know something about you, why should they give you a personal endorsement?) If you do get permission, it makes your future contacts a great deal more effective—as you'll see later on.

Your contact read your letter, does not wish to get involved, and wants to dispose of you as quickly as possible.

OK, you can't win them all. But this response doesn't mean a dead end—even if the contact refused to speak to you directly when you made your follow-up call. There are two possibilities:

Your 200 Words failed to generate the interest you were looking for. It's back to the drawing board for a bit of the third R—Review. Then, when you feel you've improved on the original, try again. There is no law against writing to someone more than once—particularly if you feel you could have presented your skills more effectively. Just modify the opening paragraph to begin:

Dear Contact,

As I explained in my last letter . . .

Your 200 Words were good, but your Contact wasn't. Remember, not everyone is a nice person. Not everyone gets a good feeling from helping other people. And some very nice people have been turned off by those who pretended to be looking for information and then wound up pressing them for a job.

Perhaps, instead of rehearsing for the phone call and sticking to the script, you tried a nervous ad-lib and it sounded that way. The result: a very crisp refusal to get involved with you, or a request for your resume—the same idea in different forms. What next? Another letter.

The greatest advantage of a letter over a phone call is that you can review every word before you use it. And you can be as direct as you like. The worst thing that can happen is that you won't get an answer. Just attach a letter like this one to a copy of your original communication:

Dear-Non-Interested-Contact:

I want to apologize for sending you the attached letter. Obviously it was a mistaken approach, and for that I'm truly sorry. But I would like to learn where I went wrong, and only you can help me.

That's why I'm taking the liberty of contacting you again in hopes of getting the information I'm looking for.

Why should you help someone you've never even met? Maybe you yourself received help at an important time in your life. Or maybe you just like the feeling that comes with lending a hand. Whatever the case, my research showed you're the ideal person to give me the information I need about the criteria by which people with my skills are hired in the aftermarket industry.

If I'm going in the wrong direction, you could tell me that. If I'm going to need additional skills, you could tell me that, as well. It won't take very long and I would be most grateful.

So can we try again? I'll call on Thursday, if I may, and set a date at your convenience.

Signed

While an honest and direct approach works more often than you think, it doesn't work all the time. And it doesn't work with everyone. If, when you call, you still get zip, write it off. But wish whoever it is a nice day.

Your contact did not read your letter and does not plan to do so.

See above.

STEP 3

Learn How to Ask the One Question that Best Initiates a **CONTACT CONVERSATION** from Which You Learn the Criteria You Must Meet to Get the Job You Want

Unlike a JOB INTERVIEW, a CONTACT CONVERSATION wears a no-stress label. This holds true for both participants. You're just looking for information about a Target field or industry. No stress. Your CONTACT LETTER was interesting enough to get you the date. No stress. There is no job at stake. No stress.

Your Contact thought you would be an interesting person to talk to and is looking forward to the conversation. No stress.

Your Contact is not being asked for a job, which he/she may not have. No stress. Your Contact is being asked for information he/she does have. No stress.

So relax.

CONDUCTING A CONTACT CONVERSATION

Thanks to TV reruns of *Red River*, even the younger generation can summon up an image of a squint-eyed Walter Brennan studying the approach of a still-distant figure and muttering to John Wayne about how he doesn't like strangers. His reason reflects the philosophy of the rugged, go-it-alone Amurrrican: "No stranger ever good-newsed me."

Unfortunately, this bug has spread. There are couples who travel only with friends so they can count on the company of known quantities. There are people who refuse invitations to places where they "won't know a soul." And every wedding party comes predivided into his or her family seating so there is absolutely no reason to talk to anyone you haven't talked to before.

What is this great fear we have of people we don't know? Old Walt resolved his uncertainties about each new face by waiting until the Duke shot him. This procedure may have relieved his tension, but it had a profoundly counterproductive effect on his networking.

Let's say it again just to make sure we understand each other. While "networking" and "broadcast letters" and "referrals" are the basic ideas, you won't find these terms in the language of the Process. Too many tricky misusers have worn out the welcome mat for them.

How to get ready to meet a stranger

The very idea of research suggests going into unknown areas, meeting unknown people, and asking them questions. Even if you had a personal introduction to Claire Good-Kind, you would be strangers to each other. Now, tell yourself the truth. Are you the kind of person who has absolutely no trouble meeting strangers? Do you feel at ease asking the kind of questions that stimulate conversation? Or do you feel awkward, find it difficult to set the right tone, and either retreat into silence or say something you're sorry for later on?

If you fit into the latter (and larger) group, don't feel bad. If asking questions makes you a bit uncomfortable, that's not surprising. Just consider the poor reputation the question has in our society. Think back to what happened in your early childhood when you were old enough to ask your first questions. The moment you did you were met with evasion:

- "Who told you to ask that question?"
- "Don't bother me now."
- "Go ask your mother (father)."
- "Wait till you're older."

When you went to school and the teacher asked a question, wasn't it clear that teach already knew the answer and was just trying to catch you?

And aren't questions the tool of unwelcome authority?

- "Where were you?"
- "How fast do you think you were going?"
- "Where are the receipts to justify these deductions?"

An obvious solution is to practice asking questions that start conversations. The next time you're at some group function where you don't know the person next to you is the ideal time to start. Forget that recurrent nightmare of a gathering at which everyone but you seems to know everyone else. Instead, look forward to the opportunity of being off in a corner with a total stranger. You have to talk to each other. So you introduce yourselves. But what's next?

What's next is a usual bit of self-conscious behavior, during which you would try to make conversation—wondering, all the while, how you let yourself get into this situation in the first place. But suppose, instead of making awkward attempts to overcome your own discomfort, you focused on the fact that the other party to your conversation may be equally self-conscious. Suppose you were able to concentrate on his/her feelings of stress rather than your own. Suppose you made it your objective to put the other party at ease. Since conversation is mandatory, practice the natural human need to communicate by asking a friendly question:

YOU: *Hi, my name is _____. I'm here because I'm an old college friend of (our host/hostess). We've been out of touch for years and just bumped into each other a few weeks ago. How about you?*

By establishing a mutual interest, this social exercise reduces the stress of getting your dialogue started. Now the conversation has a specific track on which to run.

The same mutual interest will come to your aid on Friday the 9th. Hey! That's today! At two o'clock this afternoon, guess where you'll be? At two o'clock (1:45, actually) you'll be approaching the office of Claire Good-Kind, Director, MIS Department of Aftermarket Industries.

Excited? Good. Anxious? A lot. Time is passing and you still don't have a job. And to make matters worse, that message you wrote on your bathroom mirror is getting dimmer and dimmer. Can you even remember it? "What I'm after is a job. But during the research phase of the PROCESS, what I'm after is information."

In the cold light of day it's hardly believable to you. And if you don't believe it, why should anybody else? So why not cut to the chase? If Ms. Good-Kind has been in an executive position for any length of time, she's well aware of all the job-seeking ploys that masquerade as networking. She might even come right out and say:

> Ms. G: *Bottom line, what are you after? Do you really want information about the aftermarket industry, or do you want a job?*

OK, you've got ten seconds. What's your answer? And it better be the truth. No matter how good you are at lying, nobody is that good. But which of these responses is really true for you?

> You: *I need a job. I've been out on the street for days, weeks, months, years, and I need a job. All that business in my letter about wanting to learn the criteria by which people in our specialty are hired in this industry was so much eye-wash. I really wanted a chance to meet you and to hit you up for a job.*

It could work. Just as a bolt of lightning reaches into a crowd watching a golf match and picks out a particular spectator, it could happen that Ms. Good-Kind has a job open and appreciates your candor. But more than likely she doesn't, and the bolt is fatal to your hopes.

So stay with the truth. What you want is information.

> You: *As I explained in my letter, the aftermarket industry may have a particular need for the kind of timely,*

accurate data flow I can achieve. But before I start a job-search or even write a resume, I wanted to talk to people like you who really know the industry from the inside.

If you stick to your plan, you should have no trouble explaining your purpose convincingly.

How to ask the one question you said you would ask

But suppose Ms. Good-Kind has an open mind. Your Contact Letter interested her. There you are, seated comfortably. You refuse the offer of a cup of coffee ("No thank you, perhaps later") because you'll need both hands free. And you initiate the conversation by reaching into your WORD BANK:

YOU: *Thank you for taking the time to see me, Ms. Good-Kind. As I explained in my letter, I believe the aftermarket industry may have a particular need for the kind of timely, accurate data flow I can achieve—like the branch-reporting program I designed that helped to improve productivity by twenty-five percent. But before I start a job-search or even write a resume, I want to talk to people like you who really know the industry from the inside. Out of regard for your time, may I ask just one question, make some notes, and be on my way?*

Ms. G: *I've been wondering about that.*

YOU: *By what criteria are data people like us hired in the aftermarket industry?*

Ms. G: *That's a good question. Let me think about that for a moment.*

By reaching into your WORD BANK, you are not only consistent but relaxed, since you are spared the need to ad-lib on the spur of a vital moment. The impression you make during these first few seconds will cause your Contact to decide to help you to achieve the objectives of a CONTACT CONVERSATION by:

1) Giving you the criteria by which people in your specialty are hired, so that you can create a resume that is competitive because it is right on target.

2) Referring you to other people in the industry so that you can increase your knowledge of the business as well as gain a competitive edge by expanding your network of Contacts.

3) Telling you how and where you can get the additional information or training you might need in order to better meet certain criteria.

What makes a communication between two friends work? Mutual interest, remember? Well, that's what's happening here. But we're talking about two strangers, so there has to be something more than mutual interest. And there is. It's the fact that neither party to the communication is being asked for something they would not or could not give.

As the conversation-seeker, you're perfectly willing to explain why you're someone worth talking to. Not with the story of your working life, but with the one achievement most likely to establish your bona fides—with the most important sentence borrowed from your 200 Words:

As I explained in my letter, the aftermarket industry may have a particular need for the kind of timely, accurate data flow I can achieve—like the branch-reporting program I designed that helped to improve productivity by twenty-five percent.

The conversation-seeker has to be perfectly willing to acknowledge the authority of the Contact. Not with manipulative flattery, which never fails to sound as phoney as it is, but with a statement of plain fact:

Now, while I feel that my data management skills would be applicable to the aftermarket industry, I want to talk to people like you who really know the industry from the inside. Out of regard for your time, I want to ask just one question, make some notes, and be on my way.

The very fact that your Contact has given you the appointment confirms his or her willingness to give you information. As long as that feeling continues, so will an informative, detailed CONTACT CONVERSATION.

YOU: *By what criteria are data people like us hired in the aftermarket industry?*

What makes it a good question is that Ms. G. knows the answer. As a fellow data person—hence the use of the term "us"—she knows the criteria by which she was hired, and by which her work is evaluated. And she knows the aftermarket industry from the inside.

How to make the notes

If your CONTACT CONVERSATION works out, you'll be getting a lot of vital information. And some not so vital. And some so far off the track that it's not really information at all. The problem is that there's no way to tell in advance what you should remember and what is instantly forgettable. Without competent notes, this could prove to be awkward.

Also, spin the desk and look at the situation from the Contact's point of view. Ms. Good-Kind is giving of her time and energy to give you what you said you wanted. How detailed should the information be? If you're just sitting there and making great eye contact, what's the point of loading you up with a lot of data you probably won't remember? Why not give you a few brief answers and see you out the door?

That's why have to take good notes.

Now who doesn't know how to take good notes? Most people. Not that they can't listen and write. Anybody who's been to school knows how to do that. It's simply that they never had to focus on note-taking as a competitive element in getting a job. Mind you, these same people will focus on improving a tennis stroke as if they were on the way to the Open. But note-taking? Who has to think twice about it?

Think about what kind of note-taking materials would make the best impression on the interviewer. One of those little memo pads that fit so readily inside the pocket or purse? How about a nondescript notebook? Maybe a spare sheet of paper that happened to be in your briefcase? Or, failing that, the back of one of your resumes?

Sounds like a lot about nothing, but the way you take notes sends a lot of signals to your Contact. That's why you would want to make the most professional impression by using the tools the professionals use—a **yellow, legal-size pad and a black, felt-tipped pen**. Experience has shown that because professional fact-finders use them, they command instant recognition. But a tool is only as good as its user. This means you're going to need some practice.

OK, you've just asked your question, and it's a question with which the interviewer should feel totally comfortable.

You: *Do you mind if I take some notes?*
Ms. G.: *No, not at all.*

If the information you're about to receive has any importance whatever—and the criteria by which people like you are hired certainly rates pretty high—it should be remembered

WORD FOR WORD. It should be remembered in order of importance. It should be remembered in detail. It should be expanded or explained where necessary. It should be used to create the thank-you letter. It should be used to create the Inside-Track Resume. And it should be used to demonstrate to Ms. G. that you're serious about exploring the aftermarket industry and that you're not just letting her information go in one ear and out the other.

Great! Start writing—or rather, printing.

Drawing a line down the center of the page and using the left-hand side only, BLOCK PRINT the criteria as you hear them. Block print in big letters. Letters big enough to connect the upper and lower line is the smallest size. Bigger would be even better. And leave plenty of space (about six lines) between each criterion to make additional notes which, while they don't have to be block printed, should be clear enough for you to read afterward.

If you're not wondering why all these rules apply, you should be.

The **legal-sized yellow pad** gets its designation from its official use. It sends a signal of importance. You're about to get some very important information. Your note-taking procedure should live up to it.

What's more, legal-size is big, and meets the need of printing the criteria in headlines big enough to be seen at a distance. Ms. G. will want to know that she is being noted—and quoted—correctly. The **felt-tipped pen** is not only a slick mover, but black is a highly visible color.

Very few people, and you're probably not one of them, **block print** at any great speed. This means you'll really have to concentrate on what you're doing instead of interrupting with comments of your own. You'll be focusing all your attention on what you're being told rather than on what you want to say.

This is the moment for the good listener in you to emerge and show itself. But like block printers, very few people are good listeners. To many, listening is simply the time needed to inhale before speaking. To others, listening is OK, but boring because they think they already know what they're going to hear. And, of course, there's always the temptation, upon hearing a friendly criterion, to break in with the story of your life.

But to a good listener, precisely what is being said, the order in which it is said, and the implication of what is being said are all important.

Block printing the major criteria in headline form forces you to become a good listener. Instead of a scribbled interpretation of what you're hearing (which you will be unable to read later, anyway), you're concentrating on each criterion. With some criteria, you may just get the headline. **Block print** it. With others, a story may go with it. Make supportive notes. With some, your Contact may invite discussion by asking you a question or two. Once again, a quick note summary is all you'll have time for:

Ms. G.: *It says here in your letter you're experienced in the use of the DEC VAX/ULTRIX operating system. Most of us use it, so you'd have to really be up on that.*

You: *(Repeating as you block print) UP ON DEC VAX/ ULTRIX OPERATING SYSTEM. OK, I've made a note of that. What else?*

What else, indeed? Because you're asking for more information instead of interjecting with a great story of how it was that you mastered DEC VAX/ULTRIX, here comes more information. It could be a further discussion about the operating system and how it is used. It could be a further discussion of some problems and how they are dealt with. It could be some future plans that are being considered. It could be a question about your own experience. Or it could be the next criterion.

Ms. G.: *You'd have to know how to program in C.*

You: *KNOW HOW TO PROGRAM IN C. I've noted that as well. What else?*

Ms. G.: *You would also need experience with T1 voice and communication protocol.*

You: *T1 VOICE AND COMMUNICATION PROTOCOL. I've added that. What else?*

Ms. G.: *I also see you're familiar with db-VISTA and db-QUERY. That's good. Most of the industry uses those packages for managing the data base and for running reports.*

You: *EXPERIENCE IN THE USE OF db-VISTA AND db-QUERY. OK, I've added that to the list. What else?*

Ms. G.: *Just as you described in your letter, the aftermarket business survives on fast, accurate data transfer, analysis, and reporting. If you know how to design a report that answers questions instead of provoking them, you should do OK.*

You: *KNOW HOW TO DESIGN REPORTS THAT AN-SWER QUESTIONS VS. PROVOKING THEM. Great! I've got that. What's next?*

Ms. G.: *This position calls for a lot of interface with other departments. We need their cooperation and they need ours. So you have to be a pretty good communicator.*

You: *GOOD COMMUNICATOR—INTERFACE WITH OTHER DEPARTMENTS. OK, I've got that. What else?*

Mrs. G.: *Well that's about it. Those are the key criteria.*

Your pad now has six criteria listed, with a space between each. Some of these spaces might already be filled with additional details. Others may not. So this would be a good time to stop and take stock of what you've accomplished thus far.

Not only have you introduced a topic of mutual interest that has started a low-stress conversation, but you have also gained an insider's understanding of the job criteria. Your Contact has put you on the Inside Track by verbalizing the position as she sees it, and you've done your part by listening well and taking careful notes. While an actual CONTACT CONVERSATION might result in pages of material, let's look at a simplified example:

CLAIRE GOOD-KIND, AFTERMARKET, INC. CRITERIA	
UP ON DEC VAX/ULTRIX OPERATING SYSTEM.	
KNOW HOW TO PROGRAM IN C.	
KNOW TI VOICE + COMM. PROTOCAL.	
EXPERIENCE IN USE OF db-VISTA + db-QUERY. (for managing database & running reports)	
KNOW HOW TO DESIGN REPORTS THAT ANSWER QUESTIONS US. PROVOKING THEM.	
GOOD COMMUNICATOR — INTERFACE WITH OTHER DEPARTMENTS.	

Now for a quiz. Did you think you were going to get all the way through this without one? See how many of these answers you get right—without reading ahead. (What's the point of cheating yourself?)

QUIZ

1) Why did your contact agree to see you?
   a. A mutual friend leaned on her to give you a break.
   b. She's a nice person and sees everybody who wants to see her.
   c. Your letter convinced her you were someone it might be interesting to talk to.
2) Why did your Contact have all the criteria at her fingertips?
   a. She's been planning to hire someone for her department.
   b. She stays alert to what other firms in her industry are doing.
   c. Your letter gave her a head start.
3) What happens next?
   a. You get into a deeper discussion about the criteria.
   b. She gives you the names of other people you might talk to.
   c. You thank her and leave.

The Answers:

Question 1: c is correct.

A lean-on referral (a) might get you an interview, but it will rarely get you the kind of information you're looking for. This is because a third party can rarely convince your Contact that all you want is information. Your Contact, thinking you've come for a job when she has none to give you, may have to do her friend a favor. So unless she's convinced you're someone worth talking to, she'll give you the time—but not much more.

Nobody (b) is that nice—particularly strangers who cannot give you what they think you want.

Which leaves us with (c) the quality of your CONTACT LETTER and the 200 Words from which you borrowed in order to write it. (The proof is in the next question.)

Question 2: All three are correct.

A meeting of The Association of Managers of Over-Staffed Departments could take place in a phone booth. Lean and mean is a cute slogan, but it puts one hell of a strain on the people who have to do the work. Which is why (a) it is a rare department head who isn't after his or her boss for more head-count. And the plea is often "I need somebody who can . . ."; the answer is always "Send me a memo and I'll think it over"; and the memo is usually a list of job criteria. Small wonder, then, that it's upfront in the mind of every assertive manager.

Every professional needs to stay alert to what's happening in the biz (b). One good reason is that during a period of professional musical chairs one never knows which is the next to be pulled. Another is that it pays to keep competitive with whatever is going on—thereby reducing the chance that when the music stops, an alert manager is the one who's left standing.

The proof of a good CONTACT LETTER (c) is when its contents are quoted by your Contact. The moment you hear a positive reference to your letter, it means you have a skill that is transferable to the Target field or industry.

("As it says here in your letter, you're experienced in the use of the DEC VAX/ULTRIX operating system. Most of us use it, so you'd have to really be up on that.")

If, however, this idea tempts you to construct a three-pager that describes everything you've ever done, forget it. All you've done is create a Buck-Shot Resume in letter form, which deservedly sends you back to square one.

Question 3: Once again, all three are correct.

It's virtually impossible for two people who share the same interest to avoid a friendly challenge to see who is the smartest in the land. This has to result in a deeper discussion (a) of the reason for choosing a particular approach, or the problems encountered, or the way in which a particular result was achieved. It was this collegial conversation that your Contact wanted in the first place—a chance to exchange information and ideas with somebody new.

This leads quite logically to (b) other people who might find this kind of talk to be of value.

After which it's time (c) to express your thanks and leave.

How to participate in a collegial conversation

Anyone can start it. The most natural development is for you to review the list of criteria, just in case your Contact has anything to add.

YOU: *You've been very helpful, Ms. Good-Kind. Let me review my notes of what you've told me so far:*

UP ON DEC VAX/ULTRIX OPERATING SYSTEM.
KNOW HOW TO PROGRAM IN C.
T1 VOICE AND COMMUNICATION PROTOCOL.
EXPERIENCE IN THE USE OF db-VISTA AND db-QUERY.
KNOW HOW TO DESIGN REPORTS THAT ANSWER QUESTIONS VS. PROVOKING THEM.

GOOD COMMUNICATOR—INTERFACE WITH OTHER DEPARTMENTS.

That's a great list. Are there any other criteria you can think of?

Ms. G.: *That's about it.*

If that's it, how does it look to you? For example, does the list call for what you feel are your most important skills? Remember your 200 Words?

- Developer of systems
- Reporter and evaluator of performance data
- Problem solver
- Developer of procedures
- Conductor of research
- Simplifier of reporting systems

What's more, you are able to:

- Master complex data systems
- Communicate with branch management
- Prepare manuals
- Teach and train
- Motivate
- Develop incentive programs
- Set and achieve objectives

Most important, your work delivers results:

- Productivity improved by 25%
- Error factor reduced to less than 5%

While many of your skills have already been listed—a fact which means you chose well when you targeted the aftermarket industry—how about your ability to set and achieve objectives?

YOU: *How about the ability to set and achieve objectives? Would that be a criterion?*

Ms. G.: *I hadn't thought of that, but sure—that's important.*

YOU: *Then let me add it to the list. THE ABILITY TO SET AND ACHIEVE OBJECTIVES. How about the ability to prepare manuals and to teach and train?*

Ms. G.: *Our organization has a training department that prepares materials for our dealers, but not everybody does. I know that Acme Parts doesn't. So it could be important.*

YOU: *Good. Then let me add that. THE ABILITY TO PRE-PARE MANUALS—TO TEACH AND TRAIN.*

How much time do you think has gone by? A couple of minutes for the introduction, finding seats, and refusing a cup of coffee. Perhaps a minute or two to name and note each criterion—even with a few explanatory details added that we didn't include in the script. So in under a quarter of an hour of collegial conversation you've not only made a list of six important criteria, but also added two or three of your own. This leaves you plenty of time to add more criteria to the list by drawing on more of your skills or clarifying any of the criteria you may not fully understand:

YOU: *According to my notes, you've stressed the importance of HIGH SPEED VOICE AND COMMUNICATION PROTOCOL—and you referred to the T1 in particular. I'd like to know more about that.*

Ms. G.: *Our dealers have PCs and our T1 lines are connected to a remote access data server . . . etc. etc. etc.*

Because you've established yourself as a fellow professional who wants information rather than an applicant who wants a job, this conversation has nowhere to go but up. And the more notes you take, the more interest you demonstrate, and the more information you're going to hear. Aren't you glad that you left a space under each criterion? Now your yellow pad looks like this:

CLAIRE GOOD-KIND, AFTERMARKET, INC.
CRITERIA

UP ON DEC VAX/ULTRIX OPERATING SYSTEM.

KNOW HOW TO PROGRAM IN C.

KNOW TI VOICE + COMM. PROTOCAL. (Dlrs have PC's - TI lines to remote access data server)

EXP. IN USE OF db VISTA + db QUERY. (For managing database, + running reports)

KNOW HOW TO DESIGN REPORTS THAT ANSWER QUESTIONS VS. PROVOKING THEM. (Data transfer, analysis and reporting)

GOOD COMMUNICATOR - INTERFACE WITH OTHER DEPARTMENTS.

ABILITY TO SET AND ACHIEVE OBJECTIVES.

ABILITY TO PREPARE MANUALS - TO TEACH AND TRAIN. (some organizations have training depts. Acme Parts doesn't!)

If you feel you've learned all you've come to learn or that you're in danger of wearing out your welcome—whichever comes first—it's time to live up to your promise. You asked the question about the criteria by which people in your field are hired in your Target industry. You made some notes. It's time to be on your way. But in parting, how about other people you might talk to?

> YOU: *You've been a great help, Mrs. Good-Kind. As you can see, I'm trying to decide how well my skills will fit the needs of the aftermarket industry and at what level. Is there anyone else you would suggest that I talk to? You mentioned Acme Parts, for example.*
>
> MS. G.: *That would be George Atkins, MIS Manager. I worked for him for a few years.*
>
> YOU: *Thanks. I'll drop him a note. Is it all right if I mention we spoke?*
>
> MS. G.: *Sure. Give him my regards.*
>
> YOU: *I'll do that. Is there anyone else you could suggest?*

When we wake up we'll all be back in Kansas, right? Could your CONTACT CONVERSATION really work out that way? What's that? You'll have to speak louder. That guy on the next stool is drowning you out.

> CRYER: *I knew right away that the whole idea wouldn't go down well. Who's kidding who? What I want is a job—and the sooner I get one the sooner I can start buying you drinks instead of the other way 'round.*
>
> SHOULDER: *It sounds like things didn't go too well at today's appointment. What happened?*
>
> CRYER: *No sooner did we sit down than I got this look that went right through me. And then flat out he says, "Look. What are you really after? Is it information? Or do you want a job?" So what else could I say?*

SHOULDER: *So instead of saying that you needed information, you said you were looking for a job. So what did he say?*
CRYER: *"Leave me your resume and I'll send it around." That's one I've heard before. Bartender!*

And you've probably heard it as well. Which is why, at this point, you might be thinking that the CONTACT CONVERSATION step of the process wouldn't work for you. And you could be right. But everything depends on your next word. It won't work for me *because*:

• People won't go along with that information bit.
• People don't want to get involved in my problems.
• Everyone wants to see a resume.

If experience has taught me anything at all, it's that only one thing works to unseat a well-entrenched *because*. Proof won't do it, as in: "There are case histories up the wazoo of people who used the Process and are now happily employed—some of them as a result of what started as a CONTACT CONVERSATION and ended with a job offer."

Argument won't do it, as in: "It's not as if you were being told to strip to a loincloth and perform a Zuni Indian rain dance in the reception area of a potential employer. This kind of conversation could take place with someone you met at a party, on an airplane, or even at this bar."

Logic won't do it, as in: "How do you know it won't work unless you tried it exactly as it appears in the Process?"

If you've got a really good *because* on your shoulder, the only thing that will knock it off is your own desperation. So leave a bookmark until things get tough enough and we'll catch you later.

Or do you say, it won't work for me *unless*:

• I can persuade people that I'm worth talking to.
• I can persuade people to respond to my question.
• I can persuade people that I need their information in order to write an effective resume.

That's what we've been talking about. No extra charge for re-reading and rehearsing.

THE FOLLOW-UP

Go through any Contact's mail on a given day and what will you find? Some trade periodicals, a batch of memos that either order, correct, or account for some change in plan, and bookkeeping—the invoices, purchase orders, and expense vouchers that are always late. But a friendly, personal note? Forget it. Until this:

How to send a thank-you letter

Ms. Claire Good-Kind
Director, MIS Department
Aftermarket, Inc.
123 Universe Ave.
Any City, U.S.A.

Dear Ms. Good-Kind

Thank you for your kindness and courtesy during our meeting last Thursday. I'm grateful for the information you gave me concerning the criteria by which people in data management are hired in the aftermarket industry, as well as the recommendation to contact George Atkins at Acme Parts.

I found our discussion of high-speed voice and data communication particularly helpful, since it gave me the opportunity to learn about the work being done at Aftermarket Inc. Most of all, I was very encouraged by the description of how you utilized your operating system and data packages. As we discussed, DEC VAX/ULTRIX db-VISTA and db-QUERY are an important part of my experience as well.

The work you are doing at Aftermarket Inc. sounds very productive, and while there may be no openings at the present time, I hope you will keep me in mind should an opportunity occur. Until then, as you can see by the enclosed resume, I plan to make use of your list of criteria in order to prepare myself. I'd appreciate any constructive comments.

As you suggested, I'll get in touch with George Atkins. I'll contact you, if I may, to report what happens. Thanks again.

Sincerely

The enclosure of your resume (see page 103) proves to Ms. G. that you were looking for the kind of information that would prepare you to look for a job in the automobile aftermarket industry. It also proves you were listening and that her help made a difference.

That's why you asked for permission to keep in touch. If Ms. Good-Kind has any constructive comments, you'll hear them. If she thinks of other Decision-Makers who might be interested, you'll hear about them as well. And if your potential contribution to her own department offers a higher level of productivity than she is now getting, she might be interested herself.

**How to contact the referrals you get as a result of your CONTACT
CONVERSATION**

Chances are when you contact George Atkins, he'll have some
nice things to say about Claire Good-Kind. She's a nice person.
Your report should include those comments. Nice people deserve to hear nice things about themselves.

Aside from the first sentence, your letter is the same:

Mr. George Atkins
MIS Manager
Acme Parts, Inc.
1234 5th Street
Midtown, USA 123435

Dear Mr. Atkins,

   Claire Good-Kind and I were discussing the criteria by
which data people are hired in the aftermarket industry,
and she suggested I contact you. My reason for doing so is
that after eleven years in data management, I'm looking for
a new start in a dynamic business environment. Ideally, this
would be with an organization that could make best use of
the kind of results I've achieved in gathering and analyzing
data.

   Etc.

   Between all those CONTACT LETTERS and thank-you letters and pages of notes from your CONTACT CONVERSA-
TIONS, you're becoming quite a correspondent. This means
you're going to need accurate files and records. Getting a job is
work—just like having a job is work. Good thing, too. Keeps
you in the groove.

Get the answers to any questions you may have at the halfway point

Here we are at the halfway point. The great advantage of having taught the 6-Step Job-Getting Process face-to-face for so many years was the opportunity to hear a lot of the questions that might come to mind at this juncture. Perhaps you have a few on your mind. Are they anything like these?

Q: What kind of CONTACT COMMUNICATION do you start if you want to target your own industry? After all, you can't very well say you want to talk to people who know the business from the inside if you were one of them?
A: Suppose, like our case study, you were in the mortgage department of a bank. You'd like to explore the possibilities in international leasing because you feel that's a growth area in banking. You might write:

Dear Whoever:

As you may have heard, the down-sizing at Amalgamated Bank and Trust requires that I make a new start. Ideally, this would be with some area of banking that could make best use of the kind of results I've achieved in data management.
(Then, after a paragraph that borrows from your 200 Words, your letter would continue.)
Right now I'm in the process of exploring several career alternatives. My initial research has shown that international leasing has a particular need for the kind of timely, accurate data flow that I can achieve. But before I make any decisions, I'm trying to benefit from the counsel of people like you who really know international leasing from the inside.

(The essential idea is to widen your chances by widening your horizons.)

Q: What if I can't find any articles or quotations that would give me a good lead-in for my contact letter? Suppose all I have is the name of the person in charge of that department?

A: In that case you send essentially the same CONTACT LETTER—but without the advantage that bit of research might help you to achieve:

Dear Name-But-Nothing-Else,
Manager, Data Dept.
Amalgamated Aftermarket, Inc.
123 Main St.
Midcity, USA

Dear (name),

In all my reading about the aftermarket industry, one area of information has been difficult to get at. Since my expertise is in data management, not aftermarket, I'm trying to find out how companies like Amalgamated gather and analyze the data you need to control your national distribution?

My reason for asking is that after eleven years . . . etc.

Q: What if I don't get a response?

A: You *don't* get a response. There is nothing here that suggests you wait for one, either. You *call*. Then your next step depends on the response you get. (See page 36.)

Q: If the same Contact gets a lot of letters that all sound the same, won't it be a clear sign that we're all programmed?

A: There are two answers to that question. The first is that the Contact already gets more than his/her share of exactly the same letter from people who are programmed to say: "Enclosed please find my resume" and end with "I would appreciate hearing from you." If the company is big enough to have a personnel department, that's where it's routed. If the company is small and all they have is a wastebasket, that's where it goes.

The second answer is more to the point. Eventually, as job-getting becomes more and more competitive, that flood of letters and resumes is bound to increase. This presents you with a choice. Your communication can read like the past or it can read like the present. Either way, you're going to have competition. But the more work you put into your SELF-PRESENTATION, the more interesting you become. The more interesting you become, the less competition you have.

Q: Your example shows a pretty unique situation with a very cooperative Contact. What happens when the Contact isn't that helpful?

A: While all Contacts are not equally helpful—or equally knowledgeable—the very fact that they agree to see you is a big step in the right direction. The big challenge is always the same and that is to get the meeting in the first place. Once you're there, the rest is conversation. How productive it is is up to you.

Q: What if a criterion is mentioned that you can't meet?

A: Everything depends on how important that criterion is in terms of the total job description. In the example, the second criterion was the ability to program in C. If you were the job-seeker and could meet this criterion, no problem. But what if, as a data person, you could program, but not in C?

YOU: *I notice that the second criterion is KNOW HOW TO PROGRAM IN C. Tell me more about that.*

Ms. G.: *It's another industry standard. Let me give you some of the background . . . etc.*

Once again, it's decision time. As a data person you could learn it. But when? And where? And how long will it take you? If a criterion you cannot meet keeps coming up in your Contact conversations, you've got to learn it or shift your career sights to another target.

Q: What if my Contact is at some distance—let's say in another state or even across the country?

A: Any conversation that can be conducted face-to-face can be conducted over the phone as well. OK, maybe not as well—but well enough. Remember, this is not a JOB INTERVIEW. This is a CONTACT CONVERSATION. The same question and note-taking procedure can be followed as long as your Contact has set aside enough time to provide the information you're looking for.

As a rule, a face-to-face contact makes a much better friend than a disembodied voice. However, there are a number of positive aspects to a CONTACT CONVERSATION on the telephone:

- If age, color, or physical appearance might be a limiting factor (however illegal), it won't come up over the phone.
- People tend to make their information more concise over the phone. The conversation may be shorter and not as relaxed, but you'll probably learn a lot more.
- Most important, a phone conversation can take place during or after office hours. It isn't unusual for the Contact to ask to be called at home during the evening or over the weekend. That's why your CONTACT LETTER requesting a telephone meeting should ask:

Could we talk long enough for me to ask just one question and make some notes?

If it's OK, I'll call you first thing on Thursday to set a time for our phone conversation. If that's not convenient, will you leave word with your secretary about the best time to call?

Thanks, Mr. (Ms) _____ . I appreciate it.

STEP 4

Learn How to Create a COMPETITIVE RESUME That Draws on Your WORD BANK to Match the Criteria of the Job You Want

A resume has only one objective: to get you the JOB INTER-VIEW. Even the best resume can't get you the job. So when you send a resume, what you're doing is inviting one of three responses:

- Silence.
- A form letter that thanks you for your resume but informs you that there are no openings, or, if there is an opening, that there are people in this world who fit the job in question better than you do.

- A phone call or a letter (probably the former) inviting you for a JOB INTERVIEW.

Which response you get depends a great deal on how competitive your resume is. A favorite Webster definition of competition: "The active demand of two or more organisms for some environmental resource in short supply."

That definition, converted into today's job-seeking numbers, suggests tough odds.

BEATING THE ODDS

Take 400 pieces of paper. Clip them together in pairs as if one were the cover letter and the other the resume. Fold them into thirds as if they came out of a business envelope. Unfold them. Stack them. The result is a pile of paper roughly the thickness of *War and Peace*—but not as interesting to read. That's why the Decision-Maker turns them over to a screener whose mission it is to reduce the novel to the size of a short story.

Now here's the problem. About halfway down that stack is the cover letter and resume you submitted. The screener may never get to it.

And since the screener is often from personnel or may be an administrative assistant, you can't count on his or her technical expertise in assessing your skills. For example, if the screener is instructed to look for aftermarket experience and you don't have it . . . out!

Even if the Decision-Maker takes a hand in the screening process, by the time he or she has read the first thirty-something resumes, the elapsed time spent on each gets shorter and shorter as the glaze over the eyes gets thicker and thicker.

And if you make it to the short list, your resume is now head-to-head with those submitted by people with the Inside Track.

Not a time to depend on luck. That's why this resume was prepared based on information gained during the CONTACT CONVERSATION.

J.W. Jobseeker
123 Anystreet
Mid-City, MU 12345
Telephone: (313) 445-1234

Job Objective:
   To make the best use of my 11 years of experience as a Data Manager, developing systems for reporting and evaluating performance data.

Background:
   For example, my job was to get more timely and accurate data from 24 regional management teams that were already "too busy" to submit reports even on a monthly basis. To motivate an accurate report from each office every Monday, I first developed a communication procedure to track the distribution of each element of the data. My research with branch management showed that almost a third of the data came into use only at the end of a quarter. I was able to design a modification of several data fields which simplified reporting by eliminating almost 20% of the present entries.

   To ensure cooperation, I created an operations manual and developed an incentive program. The data-system revisions and incentive program worked together to generate a weekly data flow that, according to management, helped to improve productivity by 25%. The error factor fell to less than 5%. The incentive paid for itself many times over.

To design the data gathering, analysis, and reporting program I had to master the DEC VAX/ULTRIX operating system, the db-VISTA database package, and db-QUERY language to run reports.

1981–1992: Manager, Data Department, Amalgamated Bank and Trust.

- Designed and tested computer programs in C.
- Organized data transfer systems utilizing T1 Voice and Communication Protocol.
- Designed reports that answered questions instead of provoking them.
- Interfaced with other departments to motivate cooperation.
- Set and achieved departmental objectives.
- Prepared manuals, taught systems, and trained data personnel.

1978–81: Assistant Manager, Data Department, International Pharmaceuticals.

Education: Tufts University, Medford, Mass., MBA
Personal: Complete personal data and references upon request.

Any questions? None? OK, here are some for you:

1) What is the sex of the writer? The age?
2) Why does the resume begin with an achievement rather

than getting down to itemizing the elements of the work history?

3) How did the writer select the elements of work history listed under "Manager, Data Department?"
4) Why weren't there any elements of work history listed under "Assistant Manager?"
5) Was there any work history prior to 1978?
6) In what year did the writer get the MBA?
7) Why wasn't the personal data completed?

It's important to point out that this resume wasn't designed to be admired. No fancy type faces or desk-top publishing special effects. Just the facts, ma'am (or sir). The reader can't tell (1) if you, as the writer, are male or female. This information will certainly be revealed during the interview. What should take center stage now is how well your resume meets the job criteria rather than how well you meet somebody's preconceived notion of the ideal candidate.

The story (2) borrowed from your WORD BANK is really a list of your skills. They could have been listed in the traditional menu format to look like this:

• Motivated accurate reporting
• Developed communication procedure

Pretty dull reading, isn't it? What's worse is that it looks like every one of the other hundreds of resumes. Which is why borrowing from the 200 Words to establish a professional background with an account of an important achievement offers you three competitive advantages:

• First, it's the first information the reader reads. If you believe that the first seconds are critical in making a lasting impression, how can you think of wasting time on dullness and sameness?

- Second, the account of the achievement shows *how* you work—the actual process by which you meet a challenge and deliver results. True, this information would probably come out in an interview, but it's also true that the biggest challenge is getting the interview in the first place. Showing how you work from the start can give you a competitive advantage right off.
- Last is the third-party value of the essay. Sure, your Contact would already know your story, but suppose a third party is involved—a colleague of the Contact who may have an interest but who doesn't know where you're coming from. This brief account may be the incentive to meet you and to hear more.

The criteria are listed in the order in which they were received (3). Since the resume's very first job is to accompany the thank-you letter to the Contact, it should demonstrate your ability to listen and respond.

What's the point of duplicating information under separate job descriptions on a resume (4)? Why struggle to express the exact same idea in a different way when you've already covered the topic under another title? True, this was a previous job and you're trying to show different elements of work history, but whom are you kidding? If you did essentially the same work on each job but did it well enough to advance in your field, you would do better listing the elements of the bigger job, not the lesser one(s). Of course, if there were totally different job elements involved that helped to meet totally different job criteria, they too belong in a resume. But not this one.

Who cares what happened almost fifteen years ago (5)? Unless you invented space travel back then and are looking for a job with NASA, all those bits of ancient history serve only one purpose—to prove that you're ancient.

Which is why degree dates (6) and birth dates are best left unsaid. Thanks to retirement plans, health plans, and personal bias, age has become an Intangible Criterion (see Step 5). It's illegal, but that doesn't mean it's nonexistent.

In the same way, your personal data (7)—whether you're married or single, childless or otherwise, collect stamps or are nuts about bungee jumping—can wait for the interview. You'll then have a better idea of what to mention and what to leave out.

Does any of this sound like lying? Hardly. A Contact (or Contacts) provided the information about the criteria by which people in your Target field or organization are hired. You can meet most if not all of those criteria, which is why you selected that target in the first place. You showed the criteria you can meet in your resume. That's no lie. You left out any information that was not concerned with the criteria. That's not a lie either. That's editing—under the rubric of "When writing an Inside-Track Resume, stay on the track."

How to write more than one variation of your resume

There's an Inside Track for every Target field or organization your skills might lead you to explore. While the list of criteria may be largely the same, there will probably be variations in both wording and priority. You then have a choice:

a) Write a variation of your resume to meet the specific criteria.

b) Use your standard resume but include a Procrustean cover letter.

c) Choose neither of the above and focus your job hunt on just one Target field.

If you choose (a) you're in for some extra work. But as you were warned in the opening paragraphs of this book, getting work in this market *is* work. Each variant of your resume may require an account of a different achievement in order to present a competitive background. Or you might choose to use the same achievement, but stress a different aspect of your work experience. Each variant may require a different list of job elements to meet a different list of criteria. Above all, this choice calls for keeping careful records of which resume you sent to whom so that you can recall what specific information you gave about yourself. Every word you write is true, but which truth did you tell to which reader?

The choice of (c) has such obvious limitations that there's no point in getting into it.

Which leaves us with (b) and the myth of the Procrustean cover letter. Procrustes, as you will recall from your knowledge of Greek mythology, was the son of Poseidon and not a very nice person. His claim to fame was his unique interpretation of "Bed and Breakfast." If the guest was too big for the sleeping arrangements, Procrustes simply chopped off enough of the anatomy to accommodate the bed. If the sleeper was too short, he'd stretch him till he fit.

Today, these wounds are self-inflicted by job-hunters who seek to alter their standard resumes by sending along a cover letter that tries to cut a bit here and stretch a point there. It could work, but it's working up-hill. If you're going to all that trouble, why not alter the resume itself?

Before you start complaining about all the effort involved, close your eyes. Now imagine yourself as the screener, with that stack of 200 resumes and cover letters to go through. Also on your desk is a list of the criteria by which the Decision-Maker will make the final choice so that you know what to look for.

What would you do? Would you carefully study every cover letter to see how it modifies the resume and evaluate the additional information? Or would you do a quick scan? How's that again? I didn't hear you. I was busy eavesdropping on the conversation farther down the bar:

SHE: *Sorry I'm late, but I had to come up with a short list for the new data person my boss is looking for. I must have read the same resume a hundred times or a hundred different resumes that looked the same. Right now I'm not sure.*

HE: *You look like you need a little something to cool out. Bartender!*

SHE: *There were more than 200 applicants instead of the usual 15 or so. And some heavy-weights, too, with better backgrounds than the boss has.*

HE: *Do you toss them?*

SHE: *No, but chances are the boss will. Why hire somebody as your assistant when he sounds more like your replacement? Besides, my job is to toss those that don't meet the criteria, not those who do. Oh, thanks.*

HE: *You'll feel better in a minute.*

SHE: *Some of them are so bad it makes you feel sad for the people who wrote them. Our ad said "Good communication skills." Almost a third look like ransom notes. Awful spelling. Worse grammar. "In accordance to your ad my writing and communication skills is excellent." And information crossed out or erased and changed. Into the round file.*

HE: *Who goes next?*

SHE: *Actually, it's who stays. I look for the phrases that match the phrases in our ad. The easier they are to find, the better.*

HE: *What's to stop somebody from simply paralleling your ad line for line?*

SHE: *You mean what's to start them? People pick the craziest times to get creative. We tell you the skills we're looking for. If you've got them, tell us you've got them. Tell us how you used them to get results.*

HE: *Aren't you more likely to read that in the cover letter?*

SHE: *There are more than 400 pieces of paper. With only a minute to scan each one, that's a day's work. So who reads?*

BOTH: *Bartender!*

FINDING THE RIGHT DECISION-MAKER TO READ YOUR RESUME

Imagine a situation where, instead of two or more organisms, you're the only one actively demanding the job. Your resume goes straight to the right Decision-Maker, and he or she decides that since you seem to meet the criteria there's little or no point to investing in advertising or paying a head-hunting fee. Why not just get in touch with you? Listen! Was that the phone?

As much as this idea sounds like we're on the yellow brick road to Oz, can you come up with a better cure for those piles of resumes than getting there ahead of them—or even instead of them? But it won't work, *unless*:

- During one of your CONTACT CONVERSATIONS, you hear, "We happen to have an opening coming up that we haven't even announced yet. When you've finished it, send me your resume."
- During one of your CONTACT CONVERSATIONS, you hear, "We don't have an opening right now, but we're going through a reorganization. When you've finished it, send me your resume."
- During one of your CONTACT CONVERSATIONS you hear, "We don't have an opening right now, but there's another department in our organization that might. Why don't you send your resume to . . ."
- During one of your CONTACT CONVERSATIONS you hear, "There may still be an opening at Whatzis Corp. They offered it to me, but I turned it down. Why don't you send your resume to . . ."

The uncommon denominator is that in each case your resume may be the only one. Or, if the opening is publicized, the only one that came about as the result of a CONTACT CONVERSATION, which places it neatly on the Inside Track. And on top of the stack.

How to make a list of potential readers in order of importance

Let's take the dim view. Suppose none of the above happens. Your resume, like any important piece of writing, still needs a reader, someone with an interest in what you have to say. If you were to make a list of potential readers for your resume in order of importance, it might look like this:

1) Your first Contact—the person who first told you by what criteria people in your specialty are hired in your Target field.
2) Anyone to whom your first Contact, or any subsequent Contacts, referred you.
3) Openings you heard about in your Target field that were accompanied by a personal referral to the Decision-Maker.
4) Openings you heard about in your Target field that were not accompanied by a personal referral to the Decision-Maker.
5) Head-hunters with a specific opening in your Target field.
6) Ads for specific openings in your Target field.
7) Mailings to Target organizations with no openings that you know of.

These are the basic seven, and as the numbers get higher, your chances of finding the right reader get smaller. That's why locating the right person to read your resume can take more effort than writing it. To date, no one has been able to decide which is more counterproductive—the right resume in the wrong hands or the wrong resume in the right hands. Here's the upside and the downside of each of the seven major possibilities:

First choice: Your first Contact in your Target field or organization.

The upside:

• This Contact is your first friend in the Target field or organization you're hoping to enter. He or she gave you the information you needed to write your Inside-Track Resume.
• The agreement to see you and to have a CONTACT CON-

CREATING A COMPETITIVE RESUME   113

VERSATION with you was an endorsement of your account of an important achievement. It ranked you as a
fellow professional.
- A thank-you letter for all this help is called for. Your resume is the ideal enclosure since it demonstrates your
immediate use of the valuable information you received.
- Enclosing your resume can get you constructive comment—and may generate recommendations of where to
send a copy and to whom.
- While, as your thank-you letter states, there is no opening
at the present time, you never know. If your Contact
finally succeeded in getting additional head-count, your
resume would be on top of the pile.
- People in the department may quit to take other jobs. Your
resume would be on top of the pile.
- People in the department may be terminated for not doing
as good a job as they should—or as you might. Your resume would not only be on top of the pile, but since you,
in effect, have already been interviewed, you may be the
sole applicant considered.

The downside:

- The company sounds like the ideal place to work but there
is no opening at the present time. And you can't wait. So
you go right on with your CONTACT CONVERSATIONS.

Second choice: Anyone to whom your first Contact, or any
subsequent Contacts, referred you.
The upside:

- Hearing more than one point of view makes it possible to
develop more than one variant of your resume.

- Making it a practice to enclose that resume in the thank-you letter you send to your Contact gets you the validation of its accuracy, as well as all the other possibilities already covered under "First choice."
- The more people you meet who have a personal connection with your resume, the better.

The downside:

- The pressure to get a job NOW makes you impatient with the SELF-PRESENTATION step of the process, so that when a Contact offers to distribute your resume on your behalf, you jump at the opportunity.
- Sending your resume when there is no known job opening can cost you. Barring a wonderful coincidence, what might have been a valuable CONTACT CONVERSATION with a number of positive results winds up dumped in the files or forwarded to the personnel department—whichever is worse.

Third choice: Openings you heard about in your Target field that were accompanied by a personal referral to the Decision-Maker.
The upside:

- The Contact who made the referral has read your resume and feels you're right for the job, so he or she is doing a friend a favor instead of leaning on a friend to give you a break.
- Because it is a personal referral, your resume goes directly to the Decision-Maker.
- Your resume is either on top of the stack or all alone—whichever is better.

The downside:

• There has been no personal contact between you and the Decision-Maker, so you don't know the specific criteria from his or her point of view.

Fourth choice: Openings you heard about in your Target field that were not accompanied by a personal referral to the Decision-Maker.
The upside:

• If your information is accurate, this is a bona fide job opening.
• If your Contacts have been accurate, your resume is running as close to the inside track as you can get.

The downside:

• The lack of a personal referral places you at a competitive disadvantage to those who have one.

Fifth choice: Head-hunters with a specific opening in your Target field.
The upside:

• The agency may have the exclusive listing for this job—or may even specialize in your Target field.

The downside:

• Agencies work on commission and are therefore inclined to do what they believe is most efficient: find someone with specific experience in your Target field, rather than someone with the skills to do the job.

- Like personnel departments, agencies are screeners who often lack the technical expertise needed to properly assess your skills.

Sixth choice: Ads for specific openings in your Target field. The upside:

- The fact that you took the time to research the field and construct an Inside-Track Resume stands a better chance than the general resume and cover letter.
- You can improve the odds a point or two by calling your Contacts and asking about the company (assuming the name is in the ad.) If one of your Contacts knows the organization and can refer you to the Decision-Maker, you raise the whole deal to the level of Third choice.

The downside:

- At best an ad is a long-shot—particularly if it's blind (a box number) or responses are directed to a personnel department or agency screener.
- Chances are the organization has already screened its present ranks and found somebody with the Inside Track. They're running the ad to comply with their equal opportunity procedures, or because they simply want to see "what else is out there."
- You already know about the number of responses they'll get and the level of attention each will probably receive.

Seventh choice: Mailings to Target organizations with no openings that you know of.
The upside:
There really isn't any upside. That's what makes this choice the last on the list. Despite your having the name of the

Decision-Maker, chances are that even your Inside-Track Resume will be pitched or forwarded to personnel. That's why the CONTACT LETTER asking for information stands a better chance of getting a face-to-face meeting than even a well-prepared job request when there is no job available.

How to design the proper cover letter for each potential reader

Suppose you've tried the CONTACT LETTER, or letters (page 50), and were still unable to reach your Contact. The fact that you've done a lot of homework and researched people in your Target field can now come to your rescue. A good Inside-Track Resume, like the one Claire Good-Kind and George Atkins helped you to design, is a good reason to recontact your nonresponding Contacts. The cover letter accompanying your resume explains it all:

Mr. Nonresponding Contact
World Automotive Parts
10 Industrial Park
Suburban, USA 12345

Dear Mr. Contact,

Claire Good-Kind, Director of the MIS Department at Aftermarket Industries, and George Atkins, MIS Manager at Acme Parts, Inc., were kind enough to educate me about the data-gathering needs of the aftermarket industry. The objective of my research was to determine the criteria by which people with my data background would be hired in your industry.

I approached them because, after eleven years in data management, I'm looking for a new start in a dynamic business environment. Ideally, this would be with an organization that could make best use of the kind of results I've achieved in gathering and analyzing data. (Please see enclosed.)

Right now I'm in the process of matching my skills to the criteria of aftermarket companies that have a particular need for the kind of timely, accurate data flow that I can achieve. While there may be no present opportunity at World Automotives, I'd like to prepare myself for the next opening that occurs. With that in mind, I'd appreciate an opportunity to discuss the way in which I have presented my work history and get your suggestions about any additional criteria that you feel should be added.

Could we talk long enough for me to ask just one question and make some notes? If it's OK, I'll call you first thing on Thursday to set a time for our phone conversation. If that's not convenient, will you leave word with your secretary about the best time to call?

Thanks, Mr./Ms. _____. I appreciate it.

What if (oh, happy day!) there is an opening? The third paragraph of your cover letter changes slightly—but only slightly.

Right now I'm in the process of matching my skills to the criteria of aftermarket companies that have a particular need for the kind of timely, accurate data flow that I can achieve. Since there is such a need at World Automotives, I'd appreciate an opportunity to discuss the way in which I have presented my work history and get your suggestions about any additional criteria that you feel should be added.

If it's OK, I'll call you first thing on Thursday to set a time. If that's not convenient, will you leave word with your secretary about the best time to meet?

Thanks, Mr./Ms. _____. I appreciate it.

Let's pause for a moment and say a few words about the standard cover letter. There are three basic types:

1) The Three-Liner: Acknowledges the reason for sending it—usually an ad—announces that a resume is attached, and appreciates in advance the opportunity of an interview.

2) The Procrustean: Attempts to cut or stretch the resume in an attempt to achieve a tighter fit. (See page 103.)

3) The Awkward: Adheres to the rule of thumb that says, "If you don't know what to say (since everything—and I mean everything—is said in the resume), you're bound to say something off-key."

How about a fourth variety? Now that you have an Inside-Track Resume that deals directly with the criteria of your Target field or organization, your cover letter can take credit for the research that created it.

For example, quoting the names of people or publications shows the reader that you've done your homework—a particularly important point if it is being scanned by a screener who has been instructed to look for aftermarket experience only:

Dear Decision-Maker,

Claire Good-Kind, Director of the MIS Department at Aftermarket Industries, and George Atkins, MIS Manager at Acme Parts, Inc., were kind enough to educate me about the data-gathering needs of the aftermarket industry. The objective of my research was to determine the criteria by which people with my data background would be hired in your industry.

The screener may think the Decision-Maker may know the people you're referring to. The Decision-Maker may, in fact, know the people you're referring to—and will probably know the companies. If nothing else, there may be curiosity about what the competition feels are good data-gathering criteria.

I approached them because, after eleven years in data management, I'm looking for a new start in a dynamic business environment. Ideally, this would be with an organization that could make best use of the kind of results I've achieved in gathering and analyzing data. (Please see enclosed.)

If you had any question about why your resume should begin with an account of an important achievement that showed *how* you worked rather than a chronological record that showed *where* you worked, here's your answer. You're saying a lot more than simply announcing that your resume is enclosed. Intrigued by your story, the screener may start reading rather than scanning. This could make all the difference in making it to the short list despite your lack of specific industry experience.

How to avoid the temptation to sit back and wait

You must be tired. You've made a list of the potential readers of your resume in order of importance. You've designed the proper cover letter for each potential reader. Then, making a careful record of who-got-which, you sent them out. It's at this point that your competition would be tempted to sit back and wait. But not you.

Following the same philosophy of the CONTACT LETTER, you've promised to call for an appointment. You want more than an interview. In fact the words "resume" and "interview" didn't even appear in your letters. What you want is precisely what you requested. This basic, straightforward communication asks for an opportunity to discuss how you have presented your work history, and to get suggestions about any additional criteria.

No tricks. Nothing clever or sly hidden up your sleeve. All you want to know is are there any additional criteria. There are bound to be some, as you will see in Step #5: THE JOB INTERVIEW.

STEP 5

Learn How to Conduct a **COMPETITIVE JOB INTERVIEW** That Demonstrates Your Ability to Best Meet Each of the Job Criteria

This is it—the Show. The JOB INTERVIEW. Nervous? Darn right. Look at how much work you had to do in order to come face-to-face with someone who could tell you the two most important words in the English language: You're hired.

Who can blame you, then, for forgetting everything you've learned about competitive job-getting? Who would fault you if, at this moment, you decided to become the typical applicant—nervous as hell and so eager to be chosen that you're focused completely on yourself and what you wish to achieve? Who would see anything wrong with that?

You, that's who.

Not now, of course. But if you blow this opportunity, you'll remember all the shouldas. You'll remember that instead of delivering a fascinating, thirty-minute lecture on the subject of "Every Detail of My Working Life From the Very Beginning," you shoulda focused on what the Decision-Maker was trying to achieve and how to persuade him or her that you're the one with the most skills to help achieve it.

PREPARING YOURSELF MENTALLY

As you wait for your JOB INTERVIEW you're only too aware that the rest of your working life may hang on these next few minutes. No matter how hard you try to reduce your stress level by reciting such mantras as "life goes on" and "this isn't the end of the world," that tension is there.

You may be one of those people who work best under that kind of pressure. Good for you. But as it has already been pointed out, interpersonal situations are different. Most of us become so aware of our own discomfort we completely ignore what the other party might be feeling. Since, in this case, the other party is the Decision-Maker, that kind of neglect can be fatal. Because (and this may come as a bit of a surprise to you) the Decision-Maker is as much at risk during the interview as you are.

Look at it this way. You're not coming in from the cold. You've already warmed up with a series of CONTACT CONVERSATIONS where no job was at stake. This means you're practiced in the kind of collegial discussion that results when you ask about the job criteria and note the answers.

You've taken the precaution of getting to the site of the interview with thirty minutes to spare. You've made it clear to whoever receives people that you don't wish to be announced as yet so that you could use the time to dry off if it's hot outside, warm up if it's cold outside, and to put on your game face.

You've taken a seat and reviewed your 200 Words. The very fact that your important achievement has enabled you to get face-to-face with the Decision-Maker gives you confidence. Hundreds may have applied, and you were one of the few to get this far. And you don't even have experience in the after-market industry!

But as the time approaches for the JOB INTERVIEW, riding into your otherwise sunny future come the Four Horsemen of the Apocalypse. They are nothing as dramatic as War, Famine, Pestilence, and Death. They are, instead, Rejection, Indecision, Self-Doubt and, bringing up the rear, Knocking the Opportunity.

Rejection, particularly if it is one of a series of rejections you've had lately, can be the worst. Sure, it's nothing personal. The form letter you will probably get will explain that there were others who seemed more qualified and that your resume will be kept on file.

Indecision is part of the inevitable playback that follows rejection. It begins during the elevator ride after the interview, when you begin to assess how you made out—for yourself and for other interested parties who will want to know. What did you say that would have been better left unsaid? What did you leave out that might better have been said? As the end of the week (by which time the Decision-Maker was going to call you) comes and goes, that indecision becomes magnified. Should you call the Decision-Maker? Would that be considered "pushy?" Should you continue to look for a job elsewhere? Then, what happens if this one (the one you really want) comes through?

Self-doubt sets in. Are you really as good as you think you are? Do you have all that much to offer to a potential employer? In its most advanced stage, self-doubt can lead you to wonder if you were cut out for this line of work in the first place. And all because the interview didn't go your way!

So, to defend yourself, you begin to Knock the Opportunity. It wasn't such a good job after all. Look at the commute—terrible. The neighborhood? Worse. The job itself—a dead end. And boring. And who, in his or her right mind, would want to work for that Decision-Maker? Not being chosen was the best thing that could have happened to you. (Hold on a minute—was that the phone?)

How to understand that both you and the Decision-Maker are at risk

With all that going on in your head, how could you possibly give any thought to how the Decision-Maker is at risk? To be sure, he/she is looking for the right person to fill the job. That person, once hired, would brighten the Decision-Maker's future by taking on a share of the workload, by helping to improve productivity, and might even facilitate a promotion for the Decision-Maker!

But the Decision-Maker is also hearing the oncoming hooves. Only to him/her, they are named Responsibility, Insecurity, Self-image, and Knowledge of Everything but How to Interview.

Responsibility is something that everybody has to somebody. This is never more true than when a Decision-Maker is choosing an addition to the staff. Responsibility to superiors for the quality of the decision is pretty obvious. Management may have made "recommendations" about the kind of person who should be chosen—or may have even "suggested" a name or two from among personal acquaintances or within the organization. To deviate, even for good reason, is a risk.

Then there is responsibility to those within the organization who feel *they* should have the opportunity—and have applied for it. Whoever turns them down will have to have good reason for doing so—or risk the dissension that may result. Dissension could spread the message that the Decision-Maker isn't much of a manager. And choosing the wrong person will only serve to prove it.

Which is where Indecision rears its ugly head. Does the Decision-Maker take the safe route and hire someone within the profile recommended by management—or someone with a personal recommendation, if available? That way, if the new hire doesn't work out, the Decision-Maker has an out, right? Not really. Failure is an orphan whom no one remembers having parented.

Or does the Decision-Maker choose you because you're the person best suited to help achieve the objectives he/she has in mind? That sounds logical. But what if your age, sex, color, personality, height, weight, and previous condition of servitude didn't mesh with the profile? (With all that to be considered, small wonder you weren't called by the end of the week.)

Image is what is at stake. Those who believe they are what they eat or what they wear have nothing on the organizations who feel they are whom they employ. The Decision-Maker is stuck with "how it looks," and that final word can influence the final decision.

"How does it look" if the people who report to the Decision-Maker are older, younger, of the same sex or a different sex? True, the long-term objective of every organization is to compete successfully—and this goes for both the private and public sector. But that's in the long term. For now there appears to be more concern with how you make the organization look today than how you can help it to look in the future.

That's why Knowledge of Everything but How to Interview is such a handicap in making the most productive choice. The sad fact is that most of the people who rise to Decision-Maker rank because they have been trained to do their respective jobs so well fail to see interviewing as the kind of skill that also requires training. This means that during this all-important process, which may well decide your future and that of the Decision-Maker, the matter rests in the hands of two amateurs—one on each side of the desk:

You, the Persuader	The Decision-Maker
Rejection	Responsibility
Indecision	Insecurity
Self-Doubt	Self-image
Knocking the opportunity	Knowledge of every-thing but how to interview

Add it all up and the common denominator is R-I-S-K. As the Persuader, you're at risk because you have mastered every other aspect of the job you're after except how to be interviewed for it. The Decision-Maker is at risk because he/she has mastered every other aspect of the job except how to interview you for it. In this coming together of amateurs, both sides might very well lose, unless they can come to a meeting of the minds—by developing understanding and empathy with each other. And it's not all that difficult.

How to avoid telling "all about yourself" till you know what to say

No job-seeker is the perfect choice. Therefore, every hiring is a compromise of the tangible and the intangible. The Decision-Maker is looking for someone who meets all the tangible criteria—the specific job skills required to get the work done. But there are also the intangible criteria—the personality and attitudes that "fit in." And don't forget the dollars. Management's philosophy is to try and get the best combination for the least cost. Good for them!

No job is perfect, either. And no Decision-Maker is the perfect boss. So you are looking for employment that meets all your tangible criteria—the opportunity to utilize your job skills for the best possible buck. There are also your intangible criteria—the atmosphere of the workplace, the opportunity to learn and grow, and the sense that you're making a contribution.

Obviously, some compromise on both sides is called for. So why don't you and the Decision-Maker simply match your criteria, negotiate salary and benefits, agree on a starting date, shake hands, and go out to a nice lunch?

One good guess would be that the sense of risk simply overpowers everything else. In the typical interview situation, you and the Decision-Maker go through that nervous little dance of acquaintance. An hour's wait in the reception area always helps to heighten the tension. If you're ever stuck out there so long that you think you've been forgotten, it's a sure sign you'll be meeting an untrained interviewer. It's not the delay that should tip you off. Emergencies come up in any business day. It's that no word was sent to reassure you.

But, at long last, there you are. Eager to please, you overlook the lack of apology for keeping you waiting, or smile your acceptance of the one you get. Now here comes another guess: Unless somebody says or does something to save the situation, you're in for an "off the top of the head" interview. Here's how it works:

D-M: *(Leaning back and linking hands at the top of the head) Well . . . tell me about yourself.*

YOU: *(Clearing your throat while wondering how to begin, since, in order to get the interview, you submitted a complete resume that is currently right there on the desk in front of the Decision-Maker along with ten more just like it, which is a pretty good indication that while you have achieved a place on the short list, that short list is pretty long) Well . . . I guess I'll begin at the beginning.*

You are now at maximum risk. Instead of addressing your remarks to a detailed list of the criteria required by that particular job situation, you're off on a recitation of anything and everything you think will somehow satisfy the demands of a job you really know very little about. Some of what you say may fit. Some of what you say may not. A quick look at the Decision-Maker (another guess is that while you were talking your eyes were not too well focused) will tell you how you're doing.

Is the Decision-Maker taking careful notes or are those hands still laced on top of the head? Is he/she looking at you or at the desk clock or at some papers that *really* need attention? The phone rings. The trained interviewer has already left word not to be disturbed except for some dire emergency. The phone is answered. Does the Decision-Maker refuse the call? Take it, but cut it short? Chat for a long time?

How to get on the same side of the net

The Decision-Maker who is not listening to you attentively is really hearing something else—those four horsemen. Feeling at risk, the most practical strategy for self-protection is for the Decision-Maker to try and find something in your dissertation that will disqualify you so that a safer choice will wind up with the job. Somebody with the exact industry experience. Some-

body younger. Somebody thinner. Somebody not so overquali-
fied. Somebody who looks more like they will "fit in."

D-M: *Well, that's all very interesting, but your experience
in spread-sheet evaluation won't be of much use to us,
since we use a different format.*

OK, it's your move. But where to? Out the door? On to the
next interview? Do you sit your ground and counter with a
don't-take-no-for-an-answer response that shows the Decision-
Maker the error of his/her thinking? Do you stretch a point and
invent some work experience that parallels the experience the
Decision-Maker *is* looking for? Clearly, what's happening here
is an adversarial situation.

Can't you almost see the two of you squaring off on opposite
sides of the net? The crowd is hushed as you get ready to serve
your first response to the request to tell about yourself. You
bounce several facts to see which one has the liveliest possibility. Out of the corner of your eye you see the Decision-
Maker playing deep—braced for it.

You let it go—a volley of information that seems to be right
on target. But the Decision-Maker has been on the receiving
end of many of its kind and bats it back without even a grunt.
You're down love–15 in a game that can have only one winner.

Suppose we turn the purpose of the JOB INTERVIEW
upside down. Instead of regarding the procedure as a way of
emphasizing the differences between what you are and what
the Decision-Maker is looking for, let's focus on those areas
where your goals and that of the Decision-Maker are the
same. Then the purpose of the persuasion becomes one of
demonstrating that you know what the Decision-Maker
wishes to achieve and that you are the ideal person to help
achieve it. Instead of adversaries, you're both on the same
side.

REHEARSING

The central idea is to reduce the level of risk for both parties involved in the interview. This reduces the level of stress for both of you. Remember, some compromise on both sides will be necessary.

It's your lead. For one thing, you're the stranger on the scene. For another, you've read this book and you know what to do. Most important, you're rehearsed and the Decision-Maker isn't. You took the time for a run-through—a full dress rehearsal of what you plan to say and do. You can bet the farm the Decision-Maker didn't.

For example, what is supposed to happen during the first few awkward minutes of foreplay until you are asked to tell about yourself? Who speaks? And about what? The weather? The traffic? Coffee? Remember the social conversation that explains who you are and why you're there? Imagine some invisible host has just introduced you to Mr. Deem, seen you through the hand-shake-and-have-a-seat routine, and left. You're on:

YOU: (*Opening your case and taking out your neatly arranged cover letter, resume, and yellow, legal-size pad.*) *Thank you for taking the time to see me, Mr. Deem. As I explained in the material I sent you, the aftermarket industry may have a particular need for the kind of timely, accurate data flow I can achieve—like the branch-reporting program I designed that helped to improve productivity by twenty-five percent. But to make sure, may I ask just one question?*

How to ask the one question that puts you and the Decision-Maker on the same side

As you already know, the best way to start a conversation that reduces stress is to ask a question that is easy to answer. The best way to reduce the stress on yourself is to rehearse what you're going to say and do until you at least *appear* confident and relaxed. Since the Decision-Maker knows the criteria by which he/she will select the person for this job and you wish to know them, a natural, stress-lowering question would be:

YOU: *By what criteria will you select the person for this job?*

Sound familiar? It should. It's just a slight variation on the question you asked during those Contact Conversations that led up to this interview.

Once again, you've asked a question about a topic with which the Decision-Maker should be comfortable. By doing so, you've reduced the stress. And when you reduce the stress of a JOB INTERVIEW, you reduce the R-I-S-K factor. A closer look at the structure of the question itself would reveal why:

By what criteria . . . places the focus of the discussion where it belongs—on the job, rather than on your age, sex, color, etc. What the Decision-Maker wants is someone who can do the job. Are you that someone? Can you prove it? Then that is what the discussion should be about.

. . . will you select . . . recognizes the authority of the Decision-Maker. Even if the Decision-Maker is a screener and NOT the final authority, you will need his/her approval to get to the next level.

. . . the person for this job? Unlike the CONTACT CON-VERSATION where you're asking for an industry overview,

this is an interview for a specific job. Only one person will be selected. You want it to be you.

The job criteria will fall into three basic categories:

1) The tangible criteria:

These might be the job description as expressed by your Contacts during your CONTACT CONVERSATIONS. These might be the requirements as expressed by the Decision-Maker in response to your question. Or these might be words in the ad or the job profile as given to the personnel department or the employment agency.

2) The intangible criteria:

These are not mentioned—sometimes for legal reasons. They generally relate to "the kind of people who are most likely to fit in around here."

3) The "GWS" criteria (Goes Without Saying):

These are important, but rarely if ever mentioned because they are taken for granted as the traits of any good worker. It "goes without saying" that the Decision-Maker is looking for loyalty, job dedication, high energy level, a conscientious approach to each assignment, the ability to learn quickly, etc., so nobody says it.

1) The tangible criteria can be subdivided further into two major categories: the defined and, as you might expect, the undefined. This typical advertisement demonstrates the difference between the two:

DATA MANAGEMENT SPECIALIST

Nationwide auto aftermarket co. looking for data specialist. Prior exp in VAX/ULTRIX op. sys. as well as db-Vista and db-QUERY, and T1 Voice and Communication Protocol. Programming in C a must. Candidate must be able to communicate data reports, respond to data needs of dealers, identify and implement solutions, and work under pressure situations. Exp with desk-top publishing a plus. Excel salary and co. bnfts. Equal Oppty Emp. Send resume to:

This is not a quiz, but how many tangible, defined criteria can you identify? Before you make a count, here's a hint: Use the word as it would apply to the term "tangible evidence." This means you can show specific proof of your ability to meet a defined criterion.

For example, you might offer evidence of your experience with a criterion such as VAX/ULTRIX by talking the terminology of this operating program. Or you could sit down at a computer and take it through its paces as tangible evidence of familiarity. In the same way, being able to boot up a desk-top program and produce a typical piece of output might be another proof.

Providing tangible evidence as specific proof of the ability to meet the undefined criteria might not be as possible—at least until you get some definition. Consider, for example, the innocent-looking term "communicate data reports." What does it mean? Would you be communicating these reports to one other person who would ask questions, wait for an answer, and ask for clarification if necessary? Or would the audience consist of a group of dealers who would expect a complete audio/visual presentation after which they would ask some pretty tough questions? Now, how about "respond to data needs of dealers?" What kind of data and how much of it? How many dealers and how often? And, as if that weren't enough, how would those needs be expressed?

Don't be misled into thinking that because they are undefined, these criteria are any less tangible in terms of job performance. But a description that thoroughly delineated every aspect of the job would take pages—assuming those who wrote it really knew how to define their criteria. That's why these generalities are used. That's why it's so important to determine the Decision-Maker's definitions.

Let's look at a common booby-trap like "work under pressure." Some people feel pressured if asked to do one thing at a time. Some are bored by that rate of performance. They live on impossible deadlines and will create their own if no one else does it for them. So just how much pressure you'll be working under could be an important criterion, if not the most important one.

2) The intangible criteria:

The problems of "fitting in," despite your age, sex, race, education, manner of speech, physical appearance, etc. are so important they get a special section of their own. (See page 168.)

3) The "GWS" criteria:

Every Decision-Maker expects to hire dedicated, hard-working, job-oriented people who know how to perform within company policy and complete the work on time. No doubt you see yourself as a dedicated, hard-working, job-oriented person who knows how to perform within company policy and complete the work on time. Isn't everybody? But then how is it that some people wind up carrying more of the load because some of their colleagues habitually come in late, leave early, or take lunch hours that are really mini-vacations? What makes the question even more complex is the way management reacts. Instead of listing these important work habits as part of the job criteria, they let them "go without saying." Then, after it's too late because the wrong person has been hired, they come up with warnings or incentives to correct the situation.

Hard to believe? Consider, for example, the invention of the "personal day." If you're convinced that people who tell lies don't get into heaven, you'll also believe that angels invented the personal day to make it unnecessary for perfectly healthy people to call in sick. On any given day, in ballparks, movie theaters, or just at home waiting for the plumber, are roughly a gazillion wage earners not earning their wages.

So it might be to your advantage to make what usually goes without saying *said* as part of the interview—that is, if you are indeed a dedicated, hard-working, job-oriented person who knows how to perform within company policy and complete the work on time.

How to listen to the answers and record them

Here's where you might get a little nervous. Taking notes during a CONTACT CONVERSATION is OK because you're doing research and would be expected to record the information. But at a JOB INTERVIEW? This is the one for all the marbles. Why take notes here? And suppose the Decision-Maker doesn't welcome the idea of someone taking notes?

To note or not to note is easily decided. Everything depends on whether the interview is a Type A, B, or C. Type A is an Accommodation Interview. Nobody has to take notes. Someone pleaded with the Decision-Maker to "at least have a talk" with some job-seeker. Talk is all that's going to happen.

Type B is the Basic Interview. The Decision-Maker takes notes of how each applicant responds to the basic question: "Tell me about yourself." The one who says the fewest wrong things gets the job. Since the applicant is doing all the talking, there is nothing for him/her to note.

Type C is the Criteria Interview. Both participants take notes. Since the discussion centers on the criteria for the job, the Persuader must list them to be sure to cover them all. The more persuasive his/her presentation, the more note taking the Decision-Maker will have to do to remember who said what.

Another answer can be found in the GWS criteria. It goes without saying that the Decision-Maker wants someone who is careful about understanding assignments or instructions and delivering accurate results. This means that when you get the job, you'll be expected to come to each meeting prepared to take notes. How else could you ensure careful understanding and accurate results? Taking meticulous notes during the interview demonstrates your ability to do just that.

Good note-taking also guards against interruption. The Decision-Maker, in the midst of a productive flow of ideas that you're recording, is less inclined to stop for an outside request for attention. If an interruption does occur, taking good notes can help to bring the idea flow back on track. Just recap where you were when you left off.

The safest way to determine if it's OK to take notes is to ask:

YOU: *Is it all right if I take notes?*
D-M: *Sure, go ahead.*

As always, the most direct communication is the most productive. By now, thanks to your CONTACT CONVERSATIONS and rehearsal, you're completely at ease. And thanks to your question, so is the Decision-Maker. Right now, he's considering which of the criteria listed in the job profile he filed with management, or in the ad, or with the personnel department should top the list. To give him time to do so, you're preparing your yellow, legal-size pad by block-printing the word CRITERIA on the left-hand side and drawing a line down the center of the page.

What follows, thanks to the notes made by the job-seeker involved, is an almost word-for-word transcript of an actual interview. The "almost" accounts for the fact that not every word the Decision-Maker spoke is shown. The criteria review actually took thirty minutes. What you're about to read accounts for less than half of that—note taking and all. To convince yourself, once you've read it along with the explanatory notes, turn to page 146. There you'll find the discussion in script form and without the play-by-play explanation. Read it aloud as if you were the job-getter. Practice making the notes. If you're really determined to master this step of the process in the least amount of time, get a friend to read the part of the Decision-Maker.

In the meantime, here is the Criteria Interview as it happened.

D-M: *Mainly it's getting and keeping the cooperation of our dealers. They're independents in every sense of the word and they aren't as cooperative—or as accurate—as they should be in getting the data in on time.*

Stop right there. Where did that criterion come from? Not from the ad, certainly. And not from any personnel request, either. Who would want that kind of critical comment about the dealers memorialized in an interoffice memo? It's the kind of comment one insider might make to another.

Why to you? Well, for one thing, your resume described a similar situation and how you handled it.

Why now? Perhaps it's fresh in the Decision-Maker's mind because yet another problem of that nature came up that very morning. Perhaps it's one of the reasons the previous data person couldn't cut it.

What do you do? You make note of it:

YOU: *(Repeating as you print) GETTING AND KEEPING COOPERATION OF DEALERS—GETTING DATA IN ON TIME. OK, I've made a note of that. What's next?*

And you *have* made a note of that, but from a positive point of view, without the frank, negative comments. You've just demonstrated not only your ability to get to the heart of the problem, but your tact as well.

D-M: *You have to be a strong programmer in C. While there is back-up help with a lot of the programming, you'd have to be hands-on.*
YOU: *STRONG PROGRAMMER IN C—HANDS ON. I've noted that. What else?*
D-M: *Well, the technical requirements: Knowledge of db-VISTA and db-QUERY and knowledge of T1 Voice and Communication Protocol.*
YOU: *Let me list them separately. KNOWLEDGE OF db-VISTA and db-QUERY. KNOWLEDGE OF T1 VOICE AND COMMUNICATION PROTOCOL. OK, I've listed them both. What's next?*

While the Decision-Maker might batch several criteria, there are a number of good reasons for you to list them separately—with four or five lines of space between each. The most practical of these reasons is the possibility that you might have different levels of skill for each criterion—ranging from expert to none at all. Later on, when you talk about yourself, you'll be able to make those separations work for you. You may also need the space to further define a particular criterion.

Separate listings will make it easier to take notes—and to understand them afterwards.

And the more criteria the better your chances of meeting most of them. The more you meet, the better your chances of getting the job—and the more money the job is worth.

> D-M: *Good communication skills, because you'd be making reports at our bimonthly OCM. And, of course, the dealers will be on the horn all the time asking for data.*
>
> YOU: *GOOD COMMUNICATION SKILLS—REPORT AT BI-MONTHLY OCM AND RESPOND TO DEALER DATA REQUESTS. I've made a note of that as well. What's next?*

Wait a minute. How can you make a note of something you don't fully understand, like "OCM"? You can guess it has something to do with their management system, but you're not sure. Why not interrupt the Decision-Maker's train of thought and ask for a definition? The reason is obvious. You're on a roll. Don't stop it. You can always come back for any definitions you might need later on. Remember, the more criteria, the better.

> D-M: *Well, there's no point in hiding it. This is a pressure job. When that data has to be ready it has to be ready. This means some late hours at least twice a month.*
>
> YOU: *WORK WELL UNDER PRESSURE. I've got that. And let me make an additional note that it could mean late hours at least twice a month.*

As you can see, sometimes you get the definition right along with the criterion!

D-M: I guess that's about it.

YOU: *Let me take just a moment to recap what we've covered so far. (Reading each criterion exactly as you have noted it):*

GETTING AND KEEPING COOPERATION OF DEALERS— GETTING DATA IN ON TIME.

STRONG PROGRAMMER IN C—HANDS-ON.

KNOWLEDGE OF db-VISTA AND db-QUERY

KNOWLEDGE OF T1 VOICE AND COMMUNICATION PROTOCOL.

GOOD COMMUNICATION SKILLS—REPORTS AT BI-MONTHLY OCM AND RESPOND TO DEALER DATA REQUESTS.

WORKS WELL UNDER PRESSURE.

(Late hours at least twice a month.)

Is there anything you'd care to add?

D-M: If you're familiar with desk-top publishing ... Pagemaker, Ventura, that sort of thing—it would make life a lot easier.

YOU: FAMILIAR WITH DESKTOP PUBLISHING—PAGE-MAKER, VENTURA. *OK, anything else?*

D-M: No, that's about the size of my wish list.

How to add the criteria that would balance the scale in your favor

Just as your CONTACT CONVERSATION resulted in a list of criteria by which data people are hired in the aftermarket industry, this JOB INTERVIEW has resulted in a list of criteria by which the Decision-Maker will select the person for this job. How's it going so far? Could your chances be improved by enlarging the list with a few criteria in which you are particularly strong? Once again it's time to summon up the list of skills you deposited in your WORD BANK. For example, you're rather proud of your ability to design reports, and your research has told you this could be an important skill. But the Decision-Maker hasn't mentioned it. Would that skill be important? If so, how?

> YOU: *How about report design, Mr. Deems? In my research about data gathering in the automobile aftermarket business, some industry people I talked to felt that it was important to know how to design a report that answers questions instead of provoking them. What's your feeling about that?*
>
> D-M: *Well, we talked about reporting and presenting data at the OCM—and that means answering questions. But if there's a way of designing a report that tells management what they want to know without a lot of questions, that would be a real plus.*
>
> YOU: *Then let me add that to the list: KNOW HOW TO DESIGN REPORTS THAT ANSWER QUESTIONS VS. PROVOKING THEM.*
>
> YOU: *How about systems development, Mr. Deems? Would you prefer to set the direction and have someone like myself follow through? Or do you generally delegate the design responsibility?*
>
> D-M: *You hit on a good point. I hold regular, brief staff meetings where we analyze whatever problems have come up and discuss some possible solutions. Then, whoever has to go and do it, goes and does it.*
>
> YOU: *With regular status reports back to you?*
>
> D-M: *That doesn't happen as often as I'd like.*
>
> YOU: *Let me add to the list: ABILITY TO SUGGEST AND/ OR IMPLEMENT SYSTEMS DEVELOPMENT. Then we talked about the need for a PROBLEM SOLVER. And*

third was someone ABLE TO EVALUATE AND REPORT ON PROGRESS. Is that what you had in mind?

D-M: *Could I make a photocopy of that list when we're through? I wasn't sure where you were going when we started, but we wound up with a pretty good job description.*

You: *Sure. In fact, there's just one more item. I get the feeling from what you've told me so far that this is a high-energy job . . . one that calls for someone who catches on quickly—a fast learner. Am I right?*

D-M: *Well, that goes without saying. I want someone I can depend on to get the job done.*

You: *Then that about completes the list. FAST LEARNER YOU CAN DEPEND ON TO GET THE JOB DONE. Let me make a quick recap:* (see p. 145)

How to practice, practice, practice.

Is there anyone alive who doesn't know the one about: "Can you tell me how to get to Carnegie Hall?" "Practice, practice, practice."

Good communication depends on a well-ordered flow of ideas with a minimum of distractions. The difference is most obvious during those awful interviews at intermission when the performer is asked to ad-lib. Suddenly, without a script, the air is filled with "you-knows" and "ahhhs" and "wellllls" and enough throat clearing to do credit to a ward full of respiratory diseases.

That's why the questions are handed out in advance. Practice, practice, practice. Not word for word, of course, but with enough preparation of the overall discussion to ensure that well-ordered flow. To help you do just that, here's the promised recap of the interview dialogue. Get a friend to play the

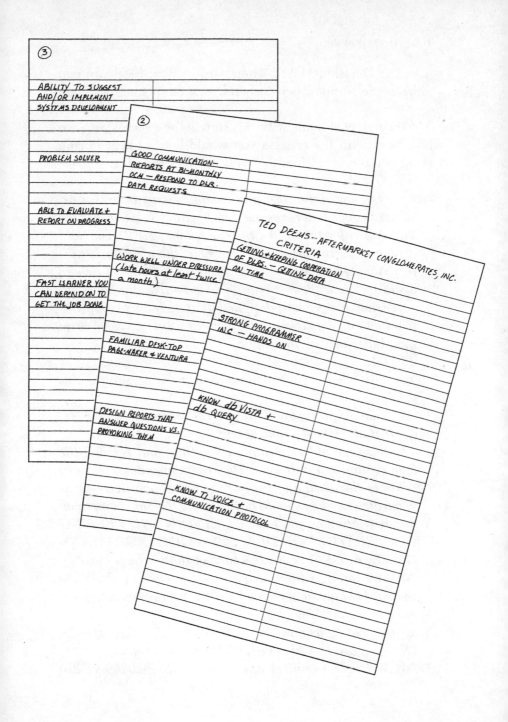

Page ③

ABILITY TO SUGGEST AND/OR IMPLEMENT SYSTEMS DEVELOPMENT	
PROBLEM SOLVER	
ABLE TO EVALUATE & REPORT ON PROGRESS	
FAST LEARNER YOU CAN DEPEND ON TO GET THE JOB DONE	

Page ②

GOOD COMMUNICATION — REPORTS AT BI-MONTHLY OCM — RESPOND TO DLR. DATA REQUESTS	
WORK WELL UNDER PRESSURE (Late hours at least twice a month)	
FAMILIAR DESK-TOP PAGE-MAKER & VENTURA	
DESIGN REPORTS THAT ANSWER QUESTIONS VS. PROVOKING THEM	

TED DEEMS—AFTERMARKET CONGLOMERATES, INC. CRITERIA

GETTING & KEEPING COOPERATION OF DLRS. — GETTING DATA ON TIME	
STRONG PROGRAMMER IN C — HANDS ON	
KNOW db VISTA + db QUERY	
KNOW TI VOICE & COMMUNICATION PROTOCOL	

part of the Decision-Maker. Then, with yellow, legal-size pad and black, felt-tipped pen in hand, practice, practice, practice.

Once you feel at home with this step of the Process, replace what's here with the criteria you would love to hear during your next interview. Then . . . well, you get the idea.

> YOU: (*Opening your case and taking out your neatly arranged cover letter, resume, and yellow, legal-size pad.*) *Thank you for taking the time to see me, Mr. Deem. As I explained in the material I sent you, the aftermarket industry may have a particular need for the kind of timely, accurate data flow I can achieve—like the branch-reporting program I designed that helped to improve productivity by twenty-five percent. But to make sure, may I ask just one question?*
>
> D-M: *OK.*
>
> YOU: *By what criteria will you select the person for this job?*
>
> D-M: *That's a pretty good question. Let me see . . .*
>
> YOU: *Is it all right if I take notes?*
>
> D-M: *Sure, go ahead. Mainly it's getting and keeping the cooperation of our dealers. They're independents in every sense of the word and they aren't as cooperative—or as accurate—as they should be in getting the data in on time.*
>
> YOU: (*Repeating as you print*): GETTING AND KEEPING COOPERATION OF DEALERS—GETTING DATA IN ON TIME. *OK, I've made a note of that. What's next?*
>
> D-M: *You have to be a strong programmer in C. While there is back-up help with a lot of the programming, you'd have to be hands-on.*
>
> YOU: (*Repeating as you print*): STRONG PROGRAMMER IN C—HANDS-ON. *I've noted that. What else?*
>
> D-M: *Well, the technical requirements: Knowledge of db-*

VISTA and db-QUERY and knowledge of T1 Voice and Communication Protocol.

YOU: *Let me list them separately. (Repeating as you print):* KNOWLEDGE OF db-VISTA and db-QUERY. KNOWL-EDGE OF T1 VOICE AND COMMUNICATION PRO-TOCOL. OK, *I've listed them both. What's next?*

D-M: *Good communication skills, because you'd be making reports at our bi-monthly OCM. And, of course, the dealers will be on the horn all the time asking for data.*

YOU: *(Repeating as you print):* GOOD COMMUNICA-TION SKILLS—REPORTS AT BI-MONTHLY OCM AND RESPONDS TO DEALER DATA REQUESTS. *I've made a note of that as well. What's next?*

D-M: *Well, there's no point in hiding it. This is a pressure job. When that data has to be ready it has to be ready. This means some late hours at least twice a month.*

YOU: WORKS WELL UNDER PRESSURE. *I've got that. And let me make an additional note that it could mean late hours at least twice a month.*

D-M: *I guess that's about it.*

YOU: *Let me take just a moment to recap what we've covered so far. (Reading each criterion exactly as you have noted it):*

GETTING AND KEEPING COOPERATION OF DEALERS—GETTING DATA IN ON TIME.

STRONG PROGRAMMER IN C—HANDS-ON.

KNOWLEDGE OF db-VISTA and db-QUERY

KNOWLEDGE OF T1 VOICE AND COMMUNICATION PROTOCOL.

GOOD COMMUNICATION SKILLS—REPORTS AT BI-MONTHLY OCM AND RESPONDS TO DEALER DATA REQUESTS.

WORKS WELL UNDER PRESSURE.

(Late hours at least twice a month.)

Is there anything you'd care to add?

D-M: *If you're familiar with desk-top publishing—Pagemaker, Ventura, that sort of thing—it would make life a lot easier.*

YOU: *FAMILIAR WITH DESKTOP PUBLISHING—PAGEMAKER, VENTURA. OK, anything else?*

D-M: *No, that's about the size of my wish list.*

YOU: *How about report design, Mr. Deems? In my research about data gathering in the automobile aftermarket business, some industry people I talked to felt that it was important to know how to design a report that answers questions instead of provoking them. What's your feeling about that?*

D-M: *Well, we talked about reporting and presenting data at the OCM—and that means answering questions. But if there's a way of designing a report that tells management what they want to know without a lot of questions, that would be a real plus.*

YOU: *Then let me add that to the list: (Saying as you print): KNOWS HOW TO DESIGN REPORTS THAT ANSWER QUESTIONS VS. PROVOKING THEM.*

YOU: *How about systems development, Mr. Deems? Would you prefer to set the direction and have someone like myself follow through? Or do you generally delegate the design responsibility?*

D-M: *You hit on a good point. I hold regular, brief staff meetings where we analyze whatever problems have come up and discuss some possible solutions. Then, whoever has to go and do it, goes and does it.*

YOU: *With regular status reports back to you?*

D-M: *That doesn't happen as often as I'd like.*

YOU: *Let me add to the list: (Saying as you print): ABILITY*

TO SUGGEST AND/OR IMPLEMENT SYSTEMS DE-VELOPMENT. Then we talked about the need for a PROBLEM SOLVER.

And third was someone *ABLE TO EVALUATE AND REPORT ON PROGRESS. Is that what you had in mind?*

D-M: *Could I make a photocopy of that list when we're through? I wasn't sure where you were going when we started, but we wound up with a pretty good job description.*

YOU: *Sure. In fact, there's just one more item. I get the feeling from what you've told me so far that this is a high-energy job . . . one that calls for someone who catches on quickly—a fast learner. Am I right?*

D-M: *Well, that goes without saying. I want someone I can depend on to get the job done.*

YOU: *Then that about completes the list. (Saying as you print): FAST LEARNER YOU CAN DEPEND ON TO GET THE JOB DONE.*

Let me make a quick recap:

GETTING AND KEEPING COOPERATION OF DEALERS—GETTING DATA IN ON TIME.

STRONG PROGRAMMER IN C—HANDS-ON.

KNOWLEDGE OF db-VISTA AND db-QUERY.

KNOWLEDGE OF T1 VOICE AND COMMUNICATION PROTOCOL.

GOOD COMMUNICATION SKILLS—REPORTS AT BI-MONTHLY OCM AND RESPONDS TO DEALER DATA REQUESTS.

WORKS WELL UNDER PRESSURE.
(Late hours at least twice a month.)

FAMILIAR WITH DESKTOP PUBLISHING—PAGEMAKER, VENTURA.

KNOW HOW TO DESIGN REPORTS THAT ANSWER QUESTIONS VS. PROVOKING THEM.

ABILITY TO SUGGEST AND/OR IMPLEMENT SYSTEMS DEVELOPMENT.

PROBLEM SOLVER.

ABLE TO EVALUATE AND REPORT ON PROGRESS.

FAST LEARNER YOU CAN DEPEND ON TO GET THE JOB DONE.

PRESENTING YOURSELF DURING THE INTERVIEW

This might be a good time to ask yourself a question: How do you feel things have been going so far? How well does what you've heard from the Decision-Maker fit your own criteria for a job you'd really enjoy, do well in, grow in, and make the kind of money you deserve?

If the opening discussion about the problems with the dealer network followed by a listing of the criteria adds up to the right job for you—great. You've taken an important step toward your new office. If you feel this job is not for you, great again. You've spared yourself and the Decision-Maker a good deal of present trouble and potential disappointment. It's time to express your thanks for the time, pack up, and be on your way.

But, once again, let's stay on the positive track. This job sounds more and more like it's right for you—pressure, overtime and all. The list of criteria looks promising enough. What you haven't already done in your previous employment you could learn to do—particularly if you're a fast learner. But you'd like to weight the scales in your favor. Don't forget the individual with the Inside Track. Don't forget the Four Horsemen and the possible decision not to make any decision at all, for fear of risking the wrong decision.

QUIZ

Since the interview and how you conduct it and yourself is so important, it's a good idea to firm up your understanding of what happens as a result of your risk-reducing behavior. If you haven't already, you may want to re-read the previous dialogue. See if you can put yourself in the place of the Persuader as you answer the following questions. Don't look at the answers until you've given each question your best shot:

1) What got you on the short list?
   a. A mutual friend leaned on the Decision-Maker to "at least have a talk with you."
   b. The Decision-Maker was deliberately looking for someone who lacked industry experience.
   c. Your resume and cover letter convinced the Decision-Maker you were someone it might be interesting to interview.
2) How was it that the Decision-Maker had all the criteria at his fingertips?
   a. He was replacing someone who had these qualifications and was promoted (or went on to another job elsewhere).
   b. He was replacing someone who lacked these qualifications and was fired.
   c. This was his new position "wish list" based on current workload requirements.

3) What happens next?
   a. You get into a deeper discussion about the criteria.
   b. You present yourself in terms of the criteria.
   c. You ask for the job.

The Answers:

Question 1: c.

Where there's an opening there's a timetable. If the work is now being done by someone who's moving on or up, that move has a date attached to it. If this is a new position it means that work that needs to be done isn't getting done. If yours was an "accommodation interview" (a) it would not rate the time needed for this kind of detailed discussion of the job criteria. In the same way (b) is possible, but not probable, because of the time that would be needed to bring a total outsider up to speed.

Which leaves us with (c) and the way in which your resume and its covering letter were, thanks to your research, riding the Inside Track. That's why the screener passed it along.

Question 2: a or b or c.

There are only two basic reasons for a job opening: replacement (a or b) or addition to the staff (c). If a replacement is being made, someone is either leaving the job or being asked to leave it. If the previous person was great, he or she left a positive imprint that management would wish to preserve. If the previous person failed at the job, he or she left a negative imprint that management would wish to correct. Either way, the Decision-Maker knows the criteria.

If management is adding to the staff it is because there is clearly more work than people who can do it. In these times, requesting new head-count is a tough sell. Chances are each talent the newcomer should add to the staff has been well thought out.

Question 3: a and b and c.

What you have here is a list of tangible criteria. (Even one GWS has been added.) Are they all clear to you? If not, there may have to be more discussion (a). To help you decide, use the following list as an example, placing a checkmark next to each criterion that you feel is clearly defined. You may not be familiar with all the terminology, but the fact is that there are certain common denominators in all criteria:

GETTING AND KEEPING COOPERATION OF DEALERS— GETTING DATA IN ON TIME.

STRONG PROGRAMMER IN C—HANDS-ON.

KNOWLEDGE OF db-VISTA AND db-QUERY.

KNOWLEDGE OF T1 VOICE AND COMMUNICATION PROTOCOL.

GOOD COMMUNICATION SKILLS—REPORTS AT BI- MONTHLY OCM AND RESPONDS TO DEALER DATA REQUESTS.

WORK WELL UNDER PRESSURE.

(Late hours at least twice a month.)

FAMILIAR WITH DESKTOP PUBLISHING—PAGEMAKER, VENTURA.

KNOWS HOW TO DESIGN REPORTS THAT ANSWER QUESTIONS VS. PROVOKING THEM.

ABILITY TO SUGGEST AND/OR IMPLEMENT SYSTEMS DEVELOPMENT.

PROBLEM SOLVER.

ABLE TO EVALUATE AND REPORT ON PROGRESS.

FAST LEARNER YOU CAN DEPEND ON TO GET THE JOB DONE.

How to define those criteria that are not entirely clear to you

For example: The term *hands-on* is clear enough. You have to be able to do it with your own hands. But what does *knowledge of* really mean? How about *familiar?*

The reason for knowing is pretty basic: you can either meet a particular criterion or you can't. Before you decide for or against yourself, it makes sense to ask for a definition:

> YOU: *According to my notes, one of your criteria calls for familiarity with db-VISTA and db-QUERY. Could you tell me why that's important?*

The Decision-Maker would then explain how the particular criterion fits into the overall job. It may be a skill that you will be called upon to use directly. It may be a skill others use under your supervision. It may be a skill other members of the team will use and would depend on your familiarity to achieve the needed cooperation. You'd want a full understanding of a criterion before you explained how well you could meet it.

In the same way, there may be "insider" terms with which you may not be familiar:

> YOU: *You said that reports would have to be made to the OCM. Could you tell me more about that?*

You might then discover that OCM stood for Office of Corporation Management, or Operations Committee Meeting or Opportunity for Critical Mention. You might learn how these groups function in the organization's decision-making system and why it is so important to present the right kind of report. Asking for more information is more effective than pretending to understand and gives you a chance to demonstrate that you're the kind of worker who would rather know than guess.

Once you're confident that you know the ground rules, you're ready to tell the Decision-Maker about yourself (b). Let the competition begin. Note: This is not a competition between you and the Decision-Maker, remember, but between you and:

- The other names on the short list.
- A delayed decision because nobody seems exactly right for the job.
- A no-decision decision that favors reorganization rather than risk hiring someone who might not be right for the job.

This means your presentation of how well you meet the criteria will need all the support you can give it—and that calls for as much proof of your abilities as you can bring to bear. Here's a checklist of just a few of the items your documentation might include:

- Letters from superiors attesting to your work habits, work skills, and work achievements.
- Documents that specifically quantify the results you've achieved: sales increased, errors reduced, time saved, business expanded, etc.
- Records of educational or work accomplishments that show you're a fast and efficient learner.
- Samples of the kind of work you've done—or can do—that best demonstrate your skills.

The Decision-Maker is looking for an individual who can meet a specific list of criteria. You happen to be an individual who can meet those criteria. In fact, you introduced a number of them yourself. Better yet, you have an excellent track record to prove it.

Now, instead of a frantic series of facts about yourself in hopes that some will hit home, you have a series of topics, each of which is of interest to the Decision-Maker. And after each topic, you ask for the job (c).

This may come as surprising news. It may come as upsetting news. Both you and the Decision-Maker know why you are there. Asking for the job should be unnecessary. You also know there are other people on the short list who are yet to be interviewed. This means the Decision-Maker is not ready to make a decision. You also know that it is the custom since the beginning of time for you to be notified "one way or another by next Thursday at the latest." So why bother asking?

What you don't know is how clearly the Decision-Maker understands the information you've just communicated. What you don't know is how accurately your information meets the particular criterion. What you don't know is whether or not the Decision-Maker has the final decision. That's why, over the door of the Temple at Karnak, in the original hieroglyphics, is an inscription that reads: "Do not pray. Ask. You have a better chance of getting an answer."

How to tell if you meet the criteria—and keep it short

You're in a great position. Don't blow it. You know the criteria by which the person will be selected for the job you're after. You seem to fill them well. They make your chances look pretty good. You've defined those criteria you may not have fully understood. You've added a few more criteria that make you look even better. The job sounds like it's right for you and you want it. You feel the Four Horsemen quietly receding into the distance. What could possibly stand between you and success?

You could. You could talk too fast—or too slowly. You could be confusing and disorganized. You could be boring. Not everyone can tell a clear, coherent, and interesting story. And some people are downright uncomfortable talking about themselves.

Not to worry. Just remember that in any effective communication, less is more. Keep it short. This means S-H-O-R-T.

Select the criterion. Start with one that would make a strong pilot for the series to follow.

Highlight the work history that best meets the criterion. For maximum impact, don't ad-lib; borrow from your 200 Words.

Offer proof. Every job-seeker makes claims. The truly competitive can prove them.

Relate your skills to the job. Show how what you have done can help the Decision-Maker to achieve what he wants done.

Test the effectiveness of your communication by asking for the Decision-Maker's reaction.

Example:

Select the criterion:

YOU: *According to my notes, an important criterion is GET-TING AND KEEPING COOPERATION OF DEALERS—GETTING DATA IN ON TIME.*

Highlight history:

As you saw in the information I sent you, I was in charge of developing systems for reporting and evaluating performance data from twenty-four regional offices. I was asked to solve the problem of getting more timely and accurate data from twenty-four regional management teams that were already too busy. I established an objective of receiving an accurate report from each office every Monday. I first developed a communication procedure to track the distribution of each element of the data and determine who was using these data and how. Thanks to my research, I was able to design a modification of several data fields that simplified reporting by eliminating almost twenty percent of the present entries.

Show proof:

Here's a diagram of the communication procedure I developed. While this may have no direct application to your own communications network, it shows my thinking and my skill at evaluating a problem.

Relate to job:

I got the feeling from what you told me that my ability to design communication systems and motivate cooperation from the field could be an important aspect to this job.

Test the effectiveness:

Am I right?

A favorite class exercise at this point in the Process was to ask everyone to close their eyes and raise their hands when they thought ninety seconds had gone by. Nobody ever gets it right. This is because ninety seconds is a lot longer than you think— particularly if, like the Decision-Maker, you're listening rather than talking.

But if you go back and read the previous paragraphs aloud at conversational speed, you'll find yourself asking that question about ninety seconds after you started. At which point you'll get one of three responses:

1) *Yes, you're right.* This is a great answer: Based on what you've presented so far, you're right for the job.

2) *Tell me more about the kind of research you did and how you went about it.* This is a great answer: Your information generated an interest in hearing more.

3) *Well, not exactly. Let me explain more about what we're looking for.* This is a great answer: While your presentation was not exactly dead center, the Decision-Maker is about to give you a chance to improve your aim. Perhaps, for example, a new system has just been put into place and your job (get the use of that expression: "your job?") would focus on motivating cooperation rather than design. No problem.

Select criterion:

YOU: *Motivating cooperation was an important part of my work.*

Highlight history:

First, I developed a manual that taught the simpler and more efficient reporting system. Then, to further motivate cooperation, I developed an incentive program of a weekend at some resort hotel within the region.

Offer proof:

Here's a copy of the manual I created and a motivational newsletter I published every month to promote both the data system and the incentive program.

Relate to job:

Motivating cooperation from the field generated a data flow that helped to improve productivity by twenty-five percent. The error factor fell to less than five percent.

Test the effectiveness:

How does that compare with what you had in mind?

Less than ninety seconds. But you're going to need the extra time to take the Decision-Maker through some of the highlights of your proof. Since part of the job calls for communication skills, here's an opportunity to demonstrate your ability to create and produce effective material. Make the most of it.

How to ask for the job each time you prove you can meet yet another criterion

Remember the only rule in this book. No tricks. No techniques. Just honest, straightforward communication between someone who wants a job and someone who wants a job done. As the Persuader, you've just explained how and why you can meet a particular criterion and proved you could do it. Now it's the Decision-Maker's turn. Does he think, based on what he's heard and seen, that you're the person he would select for this job? The only way to be sure is to ask:

YOU: *I got the feeling (this is what you wanted). Am I right?*
YOU: *(After explaining some result you achieved.) How does that compare with what you had in mind?*
YOU: *How well do you think that meets the need for someone who can (meet a particular criterion)?*

There's one catch. If you're not the kind of glib soul who never even has to pause before coming up with the exact phrase you were looking for, you're going to have to think ahead. Selecting the criterion should be no problem. You've learned them during your CONTACT CONVERSATION so you were able to anticipate many of those selected by the Decision-Maker. You were even able to add your own.

Highlighting your history was no problem because you could simply borrow from your 200 Words. Offering proof was no problem because you brought along carefully selected evidence of your skills. Relating what you could do to the needs of the job in question was no problem because you had the list of criteria right in front of you.

But the question that tests the effectiveness of what you have just said and shown may need some preparation. Here's an exercise that will help you get ready for the JOB INTERVIEW. It worked in a classroom environment for years and should work for you right now.

Imagine a dream job—one you would die for (or, to be more competitive about it—kill for.) On a page of your yellow, legal-sized pad, write a brief description of the dream job in the form of an ad or a list of criteria.

Then, select one criterion that would make you look like the dream candidate for that dream job. Word for word (borrowing from your 200 Words), write a highlight of that part of your work history that best meets the criterion you've selected.

Next, list the evidence you would show to prove you could meet the criterion.

After that, it's word-for-word time again, relating what you have said and shown to the requirement of the dream job.

And last, work out a question you would ask (or borrow one of the examples) that would test the effectiveness of what you have said and shown.

All finished? Good. Check the time on your watch. Now, taking your time, and speaking in a conversational tone, say the words aloud. When you show your evidence, don't hurry.

Point out the specific areas or information you would want the Decision-Maker to see. Allow time for looking and comprehension. After you've asked the question, check your watch again. Around ninety seconds? Good for you. You've got it.

It's even better if you become a bit compulsive. Write out a number of these criterion presentations and practice them aloud. Or you might really go off the deep end and record yourself. Then you could not only review your choice of words, but your voice quality as well. Clear? Confident? Convincing?

At this point in the Process, there are usually some questions, and these generally begin with the words "what if," as in:

Q: What if the person you're talking to doesn't know the criteria?

A: There are a number of possibilities. If the person is the screener, he or she may be responding to the "will you select" phrase in your question. That is, they know the criteria by which you make it to the Decision-Maker, but they don't know the deciding criteria because they won't be making the decision. If that happens, it's perfectly proper to amend the question to determine by what criteria people will be selected for the short list.

Another possible response is that only the Decision-Maker (generally, there's a name here—make a note of it) can answer that question. This is your opportunity to either ask what criteria will decide who gets on the short list (see above) or to ask for the opportunity to get the criteria on which the final decision will rest directly from the Decision-Maker.

Q: What if the Decision-Maker refuses to answer the question? Suppose the Decision-Maker says that he or she wishes to ask the questions—not listen to yours, and then you get the "tell me about yourself" routine?

A: You have a choice here. Remember, this is not a contest of wills with the Decision-Maker. You could take a moment to explain *why* you're asking the question:

> YOU: *I'm sorry. Perhaps I failed to make clear why I was asking that question. It was to help us both. If you tell me your criteria, you will be sure to get all the information about my background that you need. And I will be sure I cover all the essential points.*

Or you could forget all your efforts up to this point and take the chance that telling about yourself would be on target. It's your call.

Q: What if there's more than one Decision-Maker and you have to go from interview to interview as you move up the ladder? Do you ask each Decision-Maker the same question about their criteria?

A: Yes. But you let them know the results of the previous interview:

> YOU: *When I met with Mr. Deems, he was kind enough to explain the job in terms of the following criteria. (Review your notes, including the criteria you helped to add.) Is there anything you feel should be added?*

At this point, Decision-Maker #2 could choose to approve the list or add a few thoughts of his/her own. In case of the latter, you would add them to your list. Some of them may be in need of further definition, so you ask for more information. When that's done, you're ready to tell about yourself in terms of your updated list of criteria.

Q: What if the criteria have already been established by the ad or the headhunter? How could you ask about something you already know?

A: You can count on the fact that there are always more criteria than fit into an ad or head-hunter's outline. Simply follow the same JOB INTERVIEW pattern we've just discussed. This means, at the start of the interview, your yellow, legal-size pad would already have a listing (block printed with the necessary space intervals, of course) of the criteria you know about. Then it's just a matter of adding the other criteria:

YOU: *According to your ad (agency), the job calls for the following criteria. (Review your notes.) Is there anything you feel should be added?*

The Decision-Maker could approve the list as read or could add a few thoughts.

Adding your own criteria to the list:

YOU: *How about report design, Mr. Deems? In my research about data gathering in the automobile aftermarket business, some industry people I talked to felt that it was important to know how to design a report that answers questions instead of provoking them. What's your feeling about that?*

Defining the criteria:

YOU: *According to my notes, one of your criteria calls for familiarity with db-VISTA and db-QUERY. Could you tell me why that's important?*

Then, when your list is ready, so are you.

Q: What is the reason for leaving the right-hand side of the pad blank?
A: No doubt you've been wondering. The right-hand side of the pad is your control area. You use it to make sure you've covered each criterion by placing a check mark next to it as you begin. This will encourage you to refer to your notes and thereby keep the conversation on track.

> YOU: *According to my notes, you're looking for someone FAMILIAR WITH db-VISTA AND db-QUERY. (Check mark and S-H-O-R-T presentation.)*

You also use the right-hand side to note any further reaction to your presentation. For example, your question to test the effectiveness of your presentation may generate more than an approval. You may hear additional details about that phase of the job. Note them. Or, you may hear a correction of your impression of the job. Note it. The more you know about the job, the better your chance of getting it.

Q: What if everything isn't as happy valley as you suggest? What if there are criteria you can't meet so well—or at all?
A: Read on.

WHEN YOU'RE NOT PERFECT FOR THE JOB

True Story. (Everything you read in this book is true—including the request from more than one Decision-Maker for a photocopy of the job-seeker's notes. But this bit of research is even more amazing.)

As part of the background for this book, literally thousands of job criteria were screened and evaluated in terms of seemingly impossible combinations of requirements. The winner was an ad that required in-depth familiarity with super-market food merchandising, specializing in freezer inventory, display, and promotion. In addition, the applicant would need extensive experience in every phase of production and distribution of frozen fish, from the fresh catch through every step of processing, including packaging and pricing. And complete fluency in spoken and written Chinese. To cap it off, the money was not all that much.

The moral is plain. Asking ain't getting. It's the Decision-Maker's job to buy as many skills as possible for as little money as possible. Nothing wrong with that. The term "as possible" suggests an opening for negotiation.

What you want is the opportunity to place your can-do's and can't-do's in some sort of balance the Decision-Maker can weigh in comparison to those of your competition. Which is why—if you don't mind beating the obvious over the head—you ask for the criteria upfront, so you can deal with them. What you don't want are fake criteria that exist mainly in your mind or in the minds of your not-too-well-wishers which tell you that:

- "In order to get a job like that you need at least a Masters."
- "To work in the import/export environment you have to be great with languages."
- "They don't hire anyone who can't (you fill it in)."
- Surprise criteria that usually surface at the end of the interview so that the meeting ends in a negative atmosphere.
- Defensive confessions you plan to make in order to clear the air: "In all fairness I should make it clear right from the start that I'm terrible at learning foreign languages."

Instead, recite this mantra: "Thanks to my research, the contacts I made, the quality of my resume and cover letter and that God was not busy in the Middle East that week, I am on the short list. This means that while I may not meet every criteria, I have enough skills to interest the Decision-Maker in negotiating."

How to negotiate the criteria you can't meet

There are three basic ways:

1) Signal a competent, confident attitude in the way you determine the criteria by which the Decision-Maker will select the person for this job. This permits you to capitalize on that positive atmosphere in order to add enough criteria to balance those you can't meet.

2) Make the most of every criterion you *can* meet with the kind of S-H-O-R-T presentation that gets you a positive response to your test question.

3) Use each criterion you can't meet as the basis for a negotiation rather than a confession.

Suppose you were on top of every criterion in our example with one exception: You were not familiar with desk-top publishing. You recognized the names of the programs, but that was about the extent of your expertise. You have a choice. You can confess and throw yourself on the mercy of the court:

YOU: *I'm sorry, but when it comes to desk-top publishing, about all I know is the names of the programs you mentioned.*

Or, you can convert your can't-do into an opportunity to negotiate. This means that after a series of S-H-O-R-T presentations of all the criteria you could meet, you'd make an offer:

YOU: *Another criteria on your list is FAMILIAR WITH DESK-TOP PUBLISHING. From what you've learned about me so far, how long do you think it would take a person with my skills to master desk-top publishing?*

Where does the offer come in? It depends on the Decision-Maker's answer. For example, suppose the response is that all you would have to know about desk-top would be enough to edit the work of others, and that you could pick it up in a few weeks.

No offer necessary. In fact, the criterion you could not meet has been reduced in weight. The balance is easier to attain. But suppose the answer made the criterion a heavy one requiring an extensive learning curve—even for a fast learner like you. You'd have to make an offer:

YOU: *Suppose, for the three months you feel it would take for me to get up to speed, we negotiate a lower starting salary. Then, after I have mastered the system, we could review it. OK?*

How to rise above the limitations of the Intangible Criteria

The Decision-Maker who is interested in buying the most skills for the least money would find that an attractive offer. He might insist that your learning be done on your own time so that it does not interfere with your other responsibilities. He might insist you take outside training which requires that you pay a tuition. Whatever the case, most everything is negotiable.

- Even your color.
- Even your religion.
- Even your age.
- Even your sex.
- Even your physical condition.

Your personal habits—dress, hygiene, smoking, drinking or the way you blow your nose may not be, but they are too trivial to discuss here.

Don't let the phrase fool you. There ain't no such thing as "equal opportunity." Each individual in the decision-making ladder from the lowliest apparatchik in personnel to the chairman of the board has an inner image of the kind of person they feel would "fit in." In trade talk it's the "halo effect"—the tendency to endow certain characteristics with special qualities. These are generally expressed as a "they," as in:

- "We don't want a woman for this position because they . . ."
- "We're looking for a younger person because they . . ."
- "We tend not to hire Jews (or Blacks or foreign born or whatever) because they . . ."
- "We avoid overweight people because they . . ."

It's bias. In some cases, it's out and out bigotry. In all cases it's against the law. But in all too many cases, it *is* the law. And if you're overage, female, Black, foreign-born, etc., you've been that way long enough to know enough to watch the face of the Decision-Maker at the moment of first meeting. And you know what conclusion to draw.

If the Decision-Maker has the kind of poker face that could lead to wealth at a table in Vegas, there are verbal clues as well:

- There is a reluctance to answer your test questions.
- The starting date of the job is never mentioned.
- You are not asked how soon you would be available.
- You're not asked for your approval of the starting salary.

When you sense there may be an image problem, the best defense is a good offense. Who is in control—you or the bias? As you go through the social amenities, silently recite your mantra: "Thanks to my research, the contacts I made, the quality of my resume and cover letter and that God was not busy in the Middle East that week, I am on the short list. This means that while I may not meet every criteria, I have enough skills to interest the Decision-Maker in negotiating."

If you believe you're in a situation where, all other things being equal, you're not going to be chosen because you're one of "they," you have no choice. You've got to prepare for the interview so well—from determining the criteria, to the S-H-O-R-T presentation of those you can meet and the negotiation of those you can't—that the Decision-Maker will be thinking, "We really wanted someone (younger, more Wasp, lighter-skinned, etc.) for this position, but in view of your capabilities . . ."

Of course, thoughts aren't binding. Words are. So you may have to ask the Decision-Maker for the words:

YOU: *You've agreed with my capabilities in terms of (a brief review of the criteria) for which I thank you. Now, is there anything else you'd have to know about me in order to be convinced that I'm the right person for this job?*

Remember the best philosophy of good communication: Say what you mean. Is there anything else the Decision-Maker has to know in order to be convinced? If there is, he'll tell you and you can supply the information. If there isn't, he'll tell you that.

> D-M: *No. I think we've covered it all.*
> YOU: *What starting date did you have in mind?*
> D-M: *The first of the month. Are you available?*
> YOU: *Yes, I'm available for the first—assuming we can get together on salary and benefits. What starting salary did you have in mind?*

At this point you're going to hear a number which is

More than you expected:

> YOU: *That's a generous offer. I accept.*

About what you expected:

> YOU: *That sounds about right. I accept.*

Less than what you expected:

> YOU: *That's less than I expected, but I realize that I have to prove myself. When could I expect the first salary review?*

The word "convinced" is the operative one. It means just what it says. If the Decision-Maker is convinced you're the right person for the job, and the compensation package is OK with you, the job is yours—unless:

- He's not the only Decision-Maker and there are more interviews to pass.
- He feels he should see the rest of the short list.
- You're not the image and there are others to be convinced.

You'll notice that by this time the image problem has been reduced to third place. Not surprising. You're good and were able to convince the Decision-Maker that you're good. But there are other Decision-Makers on the ladder. You already know how to deal with that—starting with the notes already on your yellow pad.

YOU: *When is my next interview, and with whom?*

There are also others on the short list who are yet to be interviewed. The schedule is already set. In fact, there may be one in the reception room right at this very moment, getting ready to do what you've done. But unless the next candidate *can* do what you've done, there's nothing to worry about.

YOU: *Suppose I come back to see you some time on Thursday—just in case you have more questions. Would morning or afternoon be better for you?*

Back to image for a moment. If he's convinced that you're the person for the job but that it might be a "tough sell upstairs" or in your department, he'll need time to lay the groundwork. That can't be said, of course, so what you're more likely to hear is that he'd like you for the job but he has to think about it.

YOU: *We've reviewed the criteria and you say you're convinced I have the skills you need. Great. But I also have to fit into the working environment. The only way I can prove myself is to try it. So while you're thinking about it, how about a reasonable test period? No strings.*

That test period works both ways. You'll be able to assess what it's like to work in an environment where there are those who feel you don't fit in. Those who feel you don't fit in will have the chance to see that people with the right skills for the job are the right people for the job.

How to communicate with a Decision-Maker who is reluctant to do so

No one is quite sure how the traditional interview with its you-speak-I-listen-and-grunt format got started. Anthropologists guess that it began with the earliest man, when guttural responses were the way to go. Imagine Og optimistically leaving his cave on a job-seeking expedition, his solid-as-a-rock resume tucked safely in his Brontosaurus-skin attaché case. See him on the return trip, more than a little depressed because he failed to get any kind of positive response. You could hardly blame him if he didn't go straight home:

OG: *Bartender, a bloody Pterodactyl on the rocks. Better make it a double.*
BAR: *Hard day?*
OG: *The hardest. A job interview over at Mastodon International.*
BAR: *How'd you make out?*
OG: *How should I know? All I got out of this guy after an hour of tearing myself to shreds was a grunt or two.*
BAR: *Tough. I guess there are some people who just don't like to talk. Here, the house is buying. You look like you need another.*

What Og really needed was not another drink, but another chance. What happened—or didn't happen—was a situation as old as time. Pumped up and primed, his adrenaline in overdrive, he encountered the kind of Decision-Maker for whom every word is a commitment. So he filled the void with his own voice.

The critical moment in any interview occurs right after the social amenities—which are largely automatic speech. Now what?

YOU: *Before we begin, I'd like to ask just one question. By what criteria will you select the person for this job?*

Well done. But the Decision-Maker is silent. He doesn't provide a criterion. He doesn't even ask why you're asking. Is he thinking? If so, what about?

You ask permission to take notes. You take your time block printing the word CRITERIA on your yellow, legal-size pad. You take even more time drawing a line down the center of the page. Still nothing. You could panic and start telling about yourself. Or, you could initiate a dialogue:

YOU: *In my research about data gathering in the automobile aftermarket business, some industry people I talked to felt that it was important to know how to design a report that answers questions instead of provoking them. What's your feeling about that?*

Any question beginning with who, what, where, when, why, and how can't be answered yes or no—or with a grunt. A dialogue is now under way. If the Decision-Maker feels it's important:

YOU: *Then let me make a note of that. (Saying it as you print) THE ABILITY TO DESIGN REPORTS THAT AN-*

SWER QUESTIONS INSTEAD OF PROVOKING THEM. OK, I have that, what's next?

The Decision-Maker may tell you that, in his considered judgment, there are a number of criteria far more important than the ability to design reports. Fair enough. What are they?

Prompting a response is a great way to initiate a dialogue that will result in a list of criteria. But when you're making your S-H-O-R-T presentation and are looking for a reaction to your test question, shut up. It's the Decision-Maker's turn to talk. Wait for it. Attentively. Respectfully. Patiently. You'll get it.

Slow to talk does not mean "no."

How to negotiate a test assignment, part-time or free-lance

Even a "no" may not mean no. Everything depends on the context in which it is said. The Decision-Maker who is convinced you're right for the job but can't make a commitment at this time may still have a time problem in getting the work done. Offering to do a test assignment on a free-lance or part-time basis offers both of you a number of advantages:

The Decision-Maker:

• Gets the work done.
• Gets a chance to test your ability to do the work.
• Gets a chance to test your ability to work well with others.
• Needn't make any long-term commitments such as retirement plans, health benefits, etc.

You:

- Get a chance to see how you like the work.
- Get a chance to see how you like the working environment.
- Earn some money while you're looking for a job.
- Get a chance to amortize the cost of the business cards and stationery you had made up.

STEP 6

Learn How to Develop a
POST-INTERVIEW PROCEDURE
That Keeps the Odds in Your
Favor Despite Other Candidates
or Interviewers

In a perfect world, you would not have to read this section. You would have matched your skills to the Decision-Maker's criteria, negotiated a starting date and salary, shaken hands, and gone out to a nice lunch. What you would be reading at this point is the menu—or perhaps the wine list.

This is not a perfect world. Unless some organization is trying to seduce you away from another job—in which case you may not be desperate enough to be reading this book—the Decision-Maker is struggling with a decision that may have more layers than a Viennese torte. You cannot help but begin to feel a conflict:

- You want the job, but they want to look at other people to make sure they're making the right decision.
- They said they would let you know by Thursday, and here it is Monday and you still haven't heard.
- They said they wanted to contact your references, but you checked with your references and they told you they had heard nothing.

Where did you go wrong? Possibly nowhere. It's just not a perfect world. Unless you figure that the reason you have time to sit and wait for the phone to ring and for the angst to build is that you've quit. You have stopped your job-search. You have broken the chain of activity and left the momentum to your competition.

Don't do it. Instead, turn each of the conflict-causing statements on its head:

- *You* want to look at other jobs to be sure you're making the right decision.
- *You* want to be able to call them and say you are either considering another offer or have accepted theirs.
- *You* call your next Contact instead of your references because it is far more productive.

There is, of course, a downside to this procedure. You may wind up having to decide between two job offers. But that's what happens in an imperfect world.

When you don't walk out with a job offer

It happens. You get a great list of criteria. Your S-H-O-R-T presentation is right on the money. Even the money is right. You're feeling up. But the Decision-Maker can't make an immediate offer. There are others to see. There are superiors to consult (particularly if you're right for the job but wrong for the image).

Every up, sooner or later, is followed by a down. Newton didn't discover that, you did right after this JOB INTERVIEW. You did a great job, got all the positive responses you planned so carefully to get except the two most important words in the English language: You're hired.

It's time to go back to the wall of the Temple at Karnak where another inscription reads: "If you didn't get the offer, don't get down, get busy."

How to write a follow-up letter that outpoints the competition

Since you were planning to write a follow-up letter anyway, why not take advantage of the competitive edge you gained during the interview? Thanks to your use of the Process, the competition for the job you're after is trailing in the polls. Let's hope they didn't do as well as you did during the interview. Let's hope that, at best, they write the typical thank-you-for-the-interview letter. Let's do more than hope.

Before the term "resume" came to mean a pre-prepared, generalized work and educational history to accompany a job application, it had an identity all its own. It meant "to sum up." In French, the verb *résumer* means "to continue." Combine the two thoughts and you have the ideal follow-up letter. Not just a "thank you," but a continuation of the interview with a point-by-point summing up of what was discussed regarding the job criteria and your skills:

Mr. Ted Deems
Decision-Maker
Aftermarket Conglomerates, Inc.
12 Industrial Park
Anywhere, USA

Dear Mr. Deems,

This morning's discussion gave me a very positive view of the work I'd be doing at ACI. I trust your reaction was equally positive and that you are convinced I'm the right person for the job.

I'm enclosing a photocopy of the notes I made while we talked. It may serve as a reminder of the key points we covered. As I understood it, the most challenging part of the job would be:

- Generating cooperation from the field
- Ensuring a smooth flow of data through knowledge of db-Vista, db-Query, and T1 protocol.
- Designing and delivering reports that build the department's reputation with OCM.

From your response to my questions, I believe I explained how my skills match what you are looking for. Do you have all you need?

I would welcome further discussion to provide any other information you might require in order to confirm your decision, or to happily accept the position and clear the decks for a fast start. Would Thursday be convenient? I'll call your secretary to confirm the time.

Thank you again for the opportunity.

How badly do you want this job—not just because you need employment but because you like the work and are enthusiastic about the possibility of joining your Target organization? If you haven't communicated this information to the Decision-Maker, it's time you did. If you have, your follow-up letter serves as a reminder of that as well. It's all part of the honest, straightforward communication we've been talking about.

Our discussion of this morning gave me a very positive view of the work I'd be doing at ACI. I trust your reaction was equally positive and that you are convinced I am the right person for the job.

Not many words. Nothing fancy. You got a good feeling about the job and you want it. And you want him to want you, so you asked him to. It places particular emphasis on the key question you asked at the close of the interview: "What other information do you need in order to be convinced that I'm the right person for this job?"

I'm enclosing a photocopy of the notes I made while we talked. It may serve as a reminder of the key points we covered. I got the feeling that the most challenging part of the job would be:

- *Generating cooperation from the field*
- *Ensuring a smooth flow of data through knowledge of db-VISTA, db-QUERY, and T1 protocol.*
- *Designing and delivering reports that build the department's reputation with OCM.*

Among the many good reasons for taking good notes during the interview is that it adds strength to your follow-up letter. The average Decision-Maker, untrained in interviewing, may have more than a little difficulty trying to remember who is who and who said what. A copy of your notes not only serves as a reminder of what was discussed but gives you the opportunity to recap your key skills as well:

From your response to my questions, I believe I explained

how my skills match what you are looking for. Do you have all you need?

This also reminds him of the positive way he responded to each of your test questions and that he agreed you had the skills he needed. But he'll be reading your letter after the event—and after he has seen more of your competition. Have some comparative questions come up in his mind?

How to get another JOB INTERVIEW with the Decision-Maker if necessary

I would welcome further discussion to provide any other information you might need in order to confirm your decision, or to happily accept the position and clear the decks for a fast start. Would Thursday be convenient? I'll call your secretary to confirm the time.

Thank you again for the opportunity.

Nowhere, not even on the Temple at Karnak, is it written that there is only one interview with any particular Decision-Maker to a customer. Things may be looking good, but if there are still some questions on the Decision-Maker's mind or if he's still trying to decide between you and someone else who had made an equally good impression, what's wrong with a booster shot? And a meeting on Thursday is a lot better than a phone call promised for Thursday.

If you get the job, you can start right away to sign all the necessary forms and clear the usual red tape between you and your new desk. If you don't get the job, being there sets up the opportunity to capitalize on your contact with the Decision-Maker—even a job you don't get can lead to a job that you do get.

How to get more out of rejection than the comfort of having your name on file

It's time for your re-interview, or you have the letter from ACI in your hand or the phone is ringing. However you get your news, it's either good or bad. One rarely needs help with handling good news. It's the bad news that's sometimes hard to carry.

What makes bad news even worse is that you:

- Told everybody you know how well the interview went, even though, in the very first pages of this book, you were advised to keep this Job-Getting Process to yourself.
- Know in your heart of hearts that you didn't really stick to the Process.
- Didn't really prepare as thoroughly as you could have and it cost you.

But this is all from your point of view. What does the Decision-Maker think? What were the key factors that made him decide?

YOU: *I'm sorry to hear that. I felt the job was right for me and that I was right for it. May I ask what you thought were my strong points?*

He'll either tell you or he won't. If he does, make notes. If he doesn't:

YOU: *The reason I ask is that I'd like to learn from this experience and I'd value your advice. How do you feel I could have presented myself better? What should I have added? What should I have left out?*

And then the final question:

YOU: *As you can tell from my interest, I'm committed to making a career for myself in this industry. I gained a great deal of information during our discussion, but obviously I need more. Is there anyone you know whom I should talk to? I promise I won't use your name without your permission.*

If you're notified by letter, you send a letter:

Mr. Ted Deems
Decision-Maker
Aftermarket Conglomerates, Inc.
12 Industrial Park
Anywhere, USA

Dear Mr. Deems,

The news was bad but meeting you was good. It was probably a tough decision, and I'm sorry I won't be working for ACI right now. However, I was most impressed with you and your organization, and I would like to prepare myself for the next opportunity.

To do so, may I ask what you thought were my strong points so that I might develop them further? What additional training or preparation do you feel I need?

As you can tell from my interest, I'm committed to making a career for myself in this industry. I gained a great deal of information during our discussion, but obviously I need more. Is there anyone you know whom I should talk to in order to educate myself further? I promise I won't use your name without your permission.

Would you prefer to write me, or would it be easier to talk on the phone? I'll call you in a few days to find out.

Thanks again for your courtesy and understanding.

There's no way to anticipate every possible job-search experience. The most sensible approach, it seemed to me, short of rewriting *War and Peace*, was to deal with the most common experiences of those who have made the 6-Step Job-Getting Process an important part of their working lives over the past decade. Otherwise, this book would never be finished.

Perhaps it shouldn't be.

Working, after all, is an ongoing process. Which means looking for work is an ongoing process as well. Times get better, they get worse. Jobs change. Some begin, some end. This leads to new experiences and new "what if" questions.

As a job-seeker, you have one of three choices:

1) You can put the Process aside for now and hope for an easier way. Goodbye and good luck.

2) You can put the Process to work but introduce your own variations. I'd like to know what they are—and what happens as a result. Write to me, and tell me what happened.

3) You can put the Process to work as you see it here and make it work for you. Write to me about your new job and how you got it.

I wrote this book to help. If you've been helped, telling me how is a way of passing it on.

MONEY-BACK GUARANTEE

If you followed the 6-Step Job-Getting Process and failed to get a job offer within 60 days, return this book, *Hire Power*, along with the items listed below to:

The Zuckerman Foundation
Box 791
Larchmont, NY 10538

_____Your 200-Word Essay describing an important achievement in your career as proof of your qualifications for the job you were after.

_____Your Contact Letter

_____Your Interview Notes on the **yellow, legal-size pad** (The originals please, not a recopied version, with the date, company, and name and title of the Decision-Maker.)

_____Your copy of *Hire Power*

Please complete the following:

TO: Irv Zuckerman
Executive Director, The Zuckerman Foundation, Inc.

Dear Irv,

_____I followed your 6-Step Job-Getting Process and didn't get a job offer. Enclosed are the materials you asked for.* Please refund the purchase price of the book.

_____I followed your 6-Step Job-Getting Process and didn't get a job offer. Enclosed are the materials you asked for.* If you can figure out what went wrong and tell me how to fix it, you can keep the money. What I want is a job.

_____I got a job. Enclosed are the materials for a success story. They're all yours.

Signed _____

Name (please print) _____

Address _____Zip_____

Phone: _____Date_____

* Any returned materials become the property of the Zuckerman Foundation and may be used in subsequent publications, with names omitted or changed to disguise their source.